THE REPARATIONS PROJECT

Sarah Eisner and Randy Quarterman

THE REPARATIONS PROJECT

A Story of Friendship and Repair Work by Linked Descendants of Enslavement

The Black Studies Collection

Collection Editor
Dr Christopher McAuley

LPP

This book is dedicated to truth telling. It was written with love for the next generation, and with hope for healing in America.

First published in 2024 by Lived Places Publishing

The authors and editors have made every effort to ensure the accuracy of information contained in this publication, but assume no responsibility for any errors, inaccuracies, inconsistencies and omissions. Likewise, every effort has been made to contact copyright holders. If any copyright material has been reproduced unwittingly and without permission the Publisher will gladly receive information enabling them to rectify any error or omission in subsequent editions.

British Library Cataloguing in Publication Data
A CIP record for this book is available from the British Library

ISBN: 9781916704077 (pbk)
ISBN: 9781916704091 (ePDF)
ISBN: 9781916704084 (ePUB)

Cover design by Fiachra McCarthy
Book design by Rachel Trolove of Twin Trail Design
Typeset by Newgen Publishing UK

Lived Places Publishing
Long Island
New York 11789

www.livedplacespublishing.com

Abstract

This book tells the intertwined history and life stories of linked descendants of enslavement, Randy and Sarah, who met and developed a unique friendship and then organization. In the summer of 2019, Sarah Eisner made contact with Randy Quarterman, the great-great-great-grandson of a man, Zeike Quarterman, whom her great-great-great-grandfather, George Adam Keller, had enslaved. They quickly realized that they could work together to preserve a plot of land deeded from Keller to Quarterman in 1890 and still held by the Quarterman family but in danger of being taken by eminent domain. In this work, the two developed a close and mutually healing, as well as simultaneously challenging, friendship. This friendship enabled them to rediscover their family histories and reckon with their own individual life paths to explore the ways in which they were both similar and vastly different.

The book is written in alternating chapters by Randy and Sarah as they explore particular age points in their lives and so illustrate the ways in each of their individual experiences—both vastly different and also sometimes similar—uniquely positioned them to be able to create a community between their families and further work within broader communities toward repair.

Keywords

Reparations, personal reparations, friendship, racial repair, memoir, African American, Black studies, Black history, enslavement, racism, slavery, family, ancestry, whiteness, Georgia, Savannah, California, Bay Area

Contents

Introduction

Whiteness

As a little girl, I knew where my mother was from—where I was from—even though it was far south and east of where I was born and lived, in northern California. Forever and ever, my mother has gifted me with the sweet, gritty truth of her Savannah, Georgia roots. My roots. Sometimes these roots have been all that kept me tethered to the surface of this earth and other times they have threatened to pull me under. I don't remember a time when I didn't know that my parents and grandparents loved and cherished me unconditionally, and I don't remember a time when I didn't know that some of my ancestors—some of whom had lived long enough to love my grandmother well—had enslaved others, and I don't remember a time when that conflict wasn't part of the hole in my heart, or the opening of it. I am a cisgender woman, a mother, straight, and white, but I learned to fight against thinking that my identity is normative or black and white. I live in the questions about my family history and about the future of this country, because when it mattered most, I was encouraged by people who love me to ask them.

"Who are your people?" the Gullah Geechee people ask when one of them meets you. My mother's people are my people, even though I come from other people too: my father's Swiss family from Seattle, Washington; my mother's father's family of musicians, teachers, and Union Army soldiers from Carlinville, Illinois. But my maternal, Southern roots, running through my mother, her mother, and through all our mothers back to the 1700s are the ones I know. These are the people who have chosen me as their own, made themselves known to me, and given my life a larger purpose.

I was a college student at University of California Santa Barbara (UCSB) in 1989 when I took my first Black Studies course and asked my mother how many people our ancestors had enslaved and how much land they had owned and how could they have done so. She could not answer all these questions, but she gave me everything she knew: a lot of land, dozens of enslaved humans, and she supposed they existed within and unfortunately embraced an evil system because "that's how it was". I couldn't accept that. For two decades, as I worked my own way through school, career, and motherhood, I carried this knowledge of my family's large part in America's shame, as well as what I saw as my grandmother's conflicted Southern love, trauma, and pain, with the knowledge that I was privileged to have a family that told me the truth, and with absolute ignorance about what exactly to do with it, other than not deny or ignore it. I knew I needed to uncover it. My people inflicted pain and felt it too. I felt it. If we don't face and move through our shame and pain, we pass it down the line.

In the summer of 2019, when Ta-Nehisi Coates testified to the House of Representatives and our nation finally re-entered into semi-serious discussions about reparations for Black Americans, I didn't need to understand what, exactly, was being proposed—money, acknowledgements, land, legislation—to know in my bones that they were due. The ways in which wealth was built on the backs of Black folks but kept well out of their hands, and the ways in which slavery and its long legacy of trauma still affected us all, were facts my body carried and knew. Then, I knew it vaguely. Now, I know it more intimately.

In 2019, after a career in tech and a return to school for an MFA in creative writing, I was working on a fiction project loosely based on Harriet Keller Keller's, my great-grandmother's, life, lived with mental illness. To write the story, I tried to conjure up the place she had lived in the early part of the 1900s, Drakies Plantation, and the places her parents had lived on the nearby inland plantations, Salem and Coldbrook, both then and back to the early 1800s. I wanted to write about the ways in which I imagined "Hattie" had suffered back then that mirrored some of the ways I thought I had suffered too. The question I wanted to reckon with in writing this novel was *why* there was so much suicide, so much madness, so much eccentricity in our family history. What wounds did we suffer and hide? But working on a novel about a white girl, then a white woman—a descendant of people who had enslaved other people—"trapped" or "suffering" on a former plantation in the Jim Crow South, while I was living in Donald Trump's (or any) America felt superfluous and solipsistic, even if it wasn't. I knew that the lives of the white women in my family, and their stories, were valid and worthwhile. I knew that mine was. I even knew by then that I was, in part, writing about the ways in which white supremacy strips all people of their humanity, and often sanity, too. Maybe I just didn't think I could ever write the damn thing. I was afraid, but it was a safe fear: one of failure, not survival.

I sat at my desk in California, looking at the creamy magnolias blooming on trees outside my window in my beautiful yard. The redwood tree, taller than the whole town, lifted my gaze up to the sky and then back down. I looked at the land and thought about the land—about who owned it and why and why not and how much—and returned to the questions about the true lives of my Southern ancestors again and again, not to the fictionalization of them, as the national conversation about reparations grew. I had no delusions about who owed reparations for slavery and its legacy: the entity that created and legalized the systems that resulted in the Black–white wealth gap, the federal government, owed reparations, just as it had paid to Japanese Americans, to 9/11 survivors, to the Iran–Contra hostages, to Native Americans. But that fight had been going on for far too long. I decided I wanted to make some sort of personal reparations, a concept I naively considered I might have thought up before I learned how many people across the country were already engaging in this work. I could, at least, know my own history and tell the truth about it. I could offer up all the information I had about whom my ancestors had enslaved. I had also been lucky in Silicon Valley. I could and wanted to redistribute some of the wealth I had accumulated to those who had been held back from opportunities to accumulate it, specifically those whom my own ancestors participated in holding back more than a century ago and whose descendants had lived through slavery's legacy, one that continues today.

I started looking back through the wills I had found copies of online, reading all the family stories I could, and asking questions of the one distant cousin I knew who lived where the Kellers had lived, in Port Wentworth, Georgia. I knew him to be fascinated by family history and open hearted, and when I told him what I was trying to find he mentioned that he believed George Adam Keller had deeded two plots of land to two formerly enslaved families after the war. One plot, he thought, was given to a couple with the last name Quarterman. Bill said that Quarterman descendants still lived in town, just down the street, and he believed they also still owned the land. He didn't have their contact information. I searched them up on Google right away.

In July of 2019, I'd had no idea that the Quarterman family existed. In August, I reached out to Randy Quarterman with an email and attached the one document I had that included their family: an 1880 census that showed Isaac (called Zeike) and Grace Quarterman living on the land between two different Keller families and listed their children. Randy had not seen it before, nor the names Isaac and Grace Quarterman, and he thanked me for it, and told me he had just retired after 20 years in the military, including four tours in Iraq, and recently moved back to Port Wentworth. He also told me that yes, his family still owned most of that land given to them by George Adam Keller in 1890, but they had recently lost two acres of it to the county for a parkway by way of eminent domain, and because of the cloudy title, they had not been paid. I was stunned. I wondered: How much more would the county take? What does it mean if we allow land given to descendants of formerly enslaved people, back in 1890, to be taken away in 2019? A small spark of hope in my ancestors' humanity caught in me. Had Keller given Quarterman that land as reparations?

The truth is I had, and still have, no idea if the land my ancestor gave to Randy's family was meant as reparations or with any intent to be kind. Perhaps the land was given in exchange for a contract for completed work done *after* emancipation, additional work that hardly seems fair to require, considering the former enslavement of Zeike and Grace. Either way, I know two things are true. First, that land transfers, especially those without an exchange of money, were extremely rare from white to Black landowners in the area and that it was even more unusual to see Black women like Grace included on the deed. We could not find any other local examples of either case. And second, that even if this land was given to the Quartermans as an act of repair with no post-enslavement work as negotiation, there is no way in which this land was simply a magnanimous gift. It was hard earned. Had George Adam Keller felt that?

People often ask me whether I was afraid of the response I might get when I reached out to Randy. Of course, I was nervous. But when I honestly think about whether I was afraid, the answer is no. This is partly due to the privilege of overinflated presumption I often carry as a white woman that I am doing *the right thing*, partly due to the experiences in my life that led me to engage in deep self-reflection to be sure I *was* doing the "right" thing, and what I had taken the time to understand about what I was doing. I had taken a remarkable course called "How to Hold Whiteness Responsibly" from Laura Brewer and had begun to attend Coming To The Table meetings to learn about making connections between linked descendants. Both were key to my readiness to make a connection with Randy.

I began with humility, and quickly an apology. Although Randy (who confirmed this later) and I both understood I was not personally guilty of the offenses I apologized for, I could still start our conversation by apologizing sincerely for what people I was related to had done to people Randy was related to, *and* this apology could happen even when positive things had happened between the families too. Both families are huge and multi-branched, and each member is, of course, an individual. We both understood that none of those things negated the things I apologized for.

I knew from belonging to groups such as Coming To The Table and How to Hold Whiteness Responsibly (and I like to think also from common decency and kindness) that just reaching out to say "Hi, I'm a descendant of your ancestors' enslaver, can we talk?" was not appropriate, nor desired. I knew that I needed and wanted to offer something potentially valuable to whomever I was reaching out to rather than to ask for something that might only be valuable to me. I was lucky I had the census to offer. I was luckier still that it was Randy in particular who received it.

People often call what I did "brave". In the ways in which we've begun to call the willingness to be vulnerable "brave", it was, and I don't want to minimize the work it took to get to the point where I could reach out to the Quartermans, nor what it might feel like for other white people who decide to take similar paths. Creating human relationships, especially between those connected by generations of trauma, takes courage, and involves work and discomfort. It is also true that I hold many other kinds of bravery in higher regard. I understood that I was not in any actual physical or emotional danger when I reached out to Randy via email. I was not scared for my life or my livelihood or even of my failure. Even if the outreach hadn't gone well, it wouldn't have been me who was harmed by the intrusion or response. I simply did the best I could do with all the knowledge I could find and humility I had. Thanks to Randy, I opened myself up to rejection that never came.

I also knew that an apology or offering of a census to Randy wasn't enough: I could do more to work toward collective healing and take action. I understood quickly that doing more would be possible because of the particular person Randy is and the humane way he received me, and because of my privilege both in terms of contacts and finances, and in terms of complete support from my husband and my entire family. In the following months, as Randy and I worked together to try to find attorneys to clear title on the Quarterman land and litigate the eminent domain issue, Randy and I wrote personal narratives to swap and admire. I learned that he was born in Okinawa, Japan and had spent large parts of his earlier life there, and in Korea, Iraq, and Savannah. We discussed everything from Southern strictures to national politics, from organized religion to parenthood, and war. I began to see the threads of external and internal forces and experiences that had allowed the two of us, connected in history through enslavement and its legacy, to follow very different paths in life but to arrive, in 2019, on common ground, back where our connection began, in Port Wentworth, Georgia. As I got to know Randy's heart, I felt more optimistic about the future of America than I had in a long time, and about human connection in general. Randy echoed these sentiments, but I also knew that as we began to work together on broader goals and as we established an organization focused on racial repair, he was giving me an enormous gift at what might be a great personal cost to him. We all need healing. But Randy didn't need to make reparations. The federal government does. I felt that I, personally, could and wanted to. Randy deserved to retire from serving his country and rest. Instead, he jumped into work for the benefit of his family and for others—to serve his country in a different way—that could be retraumatizing for him and was, at best, often emotionally exhausting. That includes writing this book.

I will never be able to thank Randy Quarterman enough for answering one of the biggest questions of my life back in 2019, or for the work he has done alongside me for the past four years, or for the willingness to write our stories together. Is racial repair—are reparations for slavery and its legacy—possible? Randy and I do this work with the hope that it is, day by day, and with the understanding that we may not live to see the answer on a national scale. But reparations are a transformation, not a transaction. I am thankful for every step of both of our lives that has led us here to live in the questions and be part of a transformation together.

Learning objectives

This book tells the intertwined history and life stories of linked descendants of enslavement, Randy and Sarah, who met and developed a unique friendship and then an organization in 2019–2020. The book is written in alternating chapters by Randy and Sarah as they explore particular age points in their lives and so illustrate the ways in which each of their individual experiences—both vastly different and also sometimes similar—uniquely positioned them to be able to create a community between their families and to further work within broader communities toward repair. This story offers an opportunity to reckon with the ways in which the legacy of slavery affected descendants of two families, one Black, one white, and to see the larger systemic issues at play. Themes of societal opportunity and expectations for Americans from different socio-economic, educational, gendered, regional, and racial backgrounds are explored through the lens of the possibility for reparations in America today, both on a national scale and on an interpersonal repair scale.

1
Half

Okinawa is a small island located in the southernmost part of Japan and is known for its rich culture and history. It was also the site of a major battle during the Second World War, and the presence of the US military base, established there after the war, has been a contentious issue in the area ever since. Until 1972, the US military controlled local laws, currency, and politics throughout the Ryukyu Islands, of which Okinawa is a part. On December 5, 1975, I was born to a Japanese mother and a Black father, a combination that drew attention in both cultures. Being "half" meant that I was not full-blooded Japanese, and this was frowned upon in Japanese culture. My father was a native of Savannah, Georgia and graduated from Tompkins High School, which was an all-Black school in the period of Jim Crow segregation until the mid-1970s. In 1968, my father received a draft notification for the army and, following the advice of his father, he went to the Air Force recruiting office to sign up. He chose the Air Force because his older brother had been sentenced by a judge to join after having been found guilty of auto theft. The deal was worked out by the lawyer whom my grandmother's employer, a descendant of George Mason, found for my brother. College was not considered an option on my father's side of the family, and it's still not a priority today. The best that my family could envision was to graduate from high school and get a job at the port of Savannah or, like my father, at the Coca Cola bottling plant where he worked before being drafted.

My mother was born on Miyako Island, where the Shimoji name dates to the 1650s. However, due to the Second World War, the Shimojis became so poor that my mother never graduated high school and most of the clan migrated to Okinawa, where they became carpenters. Because not much money was put into rebuilding schools in the post-war reconstruction period in Japan, only the wealthy could send their kids to high school in Okinawa. My youngest uncle, Hideki, was the first in the family to graduate from high school in the post-war period but he still ended up going into the family's construction business. My mother was the only girl of five children. One of her brothers, who was born after her, died in childhood from pneumonia. We lit incense daily to remember him at my Ka-Chan's house at the traditional Japanese altar, which was hand crafted from wood. His cremated ashes were in a bowl where the lit incense would stand along with fresh fruits and sweets for the spirits. Ka-Chan's house always smelled like burning incense.

My parents met at a bar while my father was stationed in Okinawa as a member of the US Air Force in which he would make a 20-year career before retiring. In my father's early years in the military, he would hang out in bars off duty and enjoy Japanese night-life. Most GIs would mingle with Japanese women who would accompany men for entertainment and were paid by how much the customer would spend on drinks. I can remember as a youth walking down the lit alleys at night where women were standing and encouraging men to enter the bars and thinking, "Is this what my mother looked like, standing out here doing the same thing?" The thought made me feel ashamed and angry that my mother would do such a thing. I envisioned some drunk men passing by and my mother using her sex appeal to lure the men inside the bar. But it was my mother's decision to go into this type of work and she was young.

Around 1972 my parents fell in love and eventually got married after my father returned to Japan after station duty in Montana. My father was desperate to be stationed back in Okinawa after a year in Montana. My father felt like a man in Okinawa, where he wasn't seen by the Japanese people as "Boy" or "Nigger" but as "Scooter", a nickname given to him by the local Japanese because of his quickness on the basketball court when he played for the base team.

Still, my father had witnessed the transformation of Okinawa, which was the US military's last foothold in Japan. During the 1960s and 1970s, the Black groups that had formed within the US military during the Vietnam War started protesting and challenging the US-imposed segregation in Okinawa. Okinawans were catalyzed by the protests of Black soldiers and adopted their own protest strategies against the US military. This resulted in the Koza Riots in December 1970, which enabled the Japanese government to negotiate its reclaiming of Okinawa from the US military.

As a child, I spent much of my time with my Japanese family, learning about their customs and traditions. I attended Japanese math classes to learn *soroban*, which is an abacus developed in Japan from the ancient Chinese *suanpan*, which was imported into Japan in the 14th century. I also learned *shodo*, a Japanese calligraphy, which was like a high art class. The *shodo* teachers were very strict and would often scold me for not dedicating myself to it. Finally, there was karate class, which I only did to be a part of something when all I really wanted to do was to play outside with my friends. What I didn't want to do was stay at home alone.

My grandmother, whom I called Ka-Chan, taught me the importance of respect, discipline, and perseverance, which were values that would later shape my character. She took the time to show me the ways of life, whether it was just showing me how to pick the right sashimi at the fish market and testing me the next week by having me choose the fish. She was the person who really explained Japanese culture to me, which is based more on body language than is American culture. Although I only spent a few weekends a month with her, I could tell that she just enjoyed my company.

My uncles, Hideki and Shungi, who were only about 10–15 years older than me, also looked after me and gave me some of the happiest times of my life. They would take me everywhere—to the beach, amusement parks, on drives across Okinawa—and just allowed me to be part of their lives.

I also had a strong connection to my father's culture, especially through his love of music. My father would often play soul music by performers like Marvin Gaye and Earth Wind and Fire, and, for jazz records, he listened to a lot of Spyro Gyra. We would dance together in our living room, being entirely free-spirited. It was a feeling that I can't put a name to, but it was the effect of the rhythms that the musicians created with their instruments and voices. I never knew about my father's experiences in America as a Black man, nor did I know of his hurdles and struggles, which he wanted to protect me from.

My father would always tell me that, as a child of the segregated South, all he wanted for me was the "freedom" to be a child without any boundaries. There is one story that I remember him telling me that makes me cringe a little since I am a parent. He told me that when I was about two or three years old, I was outside playing and eventually drifted off so far from home that a strange woman saw me and went looking for my parents since they were the only interracial couple in the area. This was evidence of my adventurous and naïve nature and that my father got his wish for me. I was also a kid with a deep sense of empathy and loyalty.

It was around July 1979, when my father received his next assignment, that I got my introduction to America and its culture. The air smelled like salt from the ocean and the sun was bright as a summer. The cicadas in the trees that all the kids would try to catch were making their buzzing noise. While I was outside climbing trees, my parents were inside with the movers packing for our next destination, Albuquerque, New Mexico, where father was assigned for 18 months. What I can remember is Ka-chan and my parents waiting for our flight at Kadena Airport. This was the first time I was getting on an airplane, so I was very excited and not thinking about the changes that were about to occur. Our first destination prior to New Mexico was my father's hometown of Savannah, Georgia, where I would be amid his family and culture. This would be my first time around my Black family.

At this point I was unable to speak English, so the only person whom I could communicate with was my mother. My father was there to translate the best that he could to his family, but considering that my household was not a very vocal one, which was normal in Japanese culture, he did not have much to translate from us. Silence in conversation is quite commonplace in Japan, where people read between the lines and understand others through non-verbal cues, like context, body language, and other such social indicators. This training gave me a way to navigate this new world, but it didn't always help me to understand Black American culture.

This was the first time I saw so many Black folks in one area. Being with Black people was not an entirely new experience to me because my father had Black friends in Okinawa. However, this would be my first time around Black people for 24 hours a day and 7 days a week. I can remember the gathering over dinner and thinking to myself about how much meat there was on the table and how big some of the adults were. In Japan you were ridiculed if you were overweight. Also, we didn't have individual plates in Japan but shared the entrée among ourselves. The only individual dish we had were our soup and rice bowls. Seeing how my family ate made me feel even more out of place. I could only look to my mother for guidance, and she always looked to father for some.

I can remember my aunts advising my mother to take more of an assertive role as a wife but what they didn't understand was that my mother's behavior, which they took as submissive, was simply that of a Japanese woman at the time. I could see in my mother's eyes that she didn't enjoy any part of the US but she supported me and my father because she understood that this was our culture as well.

I would often hear my paternal grandmother tell my father that I was "wild", a word that I didn't understand at that time but would later realize that she meant that I was untamable or free-spirited. One evening I heard my cousin getting into trouble and saw him being disciplined with a belt. This was the first time that I had ever seen anything like this, and I was so afraid that I ran to my mother and asked her why this was happening and if I would be next. I can remember my mother's reaction to this event and how it was a total shock to her, too. I cried in her lap as she held me tightly. Other than that experience, I remember the visit with my father's family as more of an adventure for me at four years old than anything else.

I was my mother's only child, and I felt the emptiness of not having siblings. I would carry this feeling into adulthood. What I learned from our visit to Savannah was that I had an older brother and older sister, but I didn't understand why they did not live with us. I did not question my father about this. My siblings were six to ten years older than me and, unlike me who was half-Black, they were fully Black. I felt like I was constantly walking a tightrope between my two identities, never fully belonging to either. My childhood was filled with confusion, questions, and curiosity about my unique background.

After a week or two of visiting my family in Carver Village, which was once known as the largest individually owned housing development for people of color in the world, with over 600 homes, we traveled to New Mexico. We drove there in a 1973

Grand Prix that my father bought in Montana, where he was stationed before I was born. I thought it was the biggest car I had ever seen, and it would be our home for the next few days as we made our way across the country. Being on the road and seeing all this land was an adventurous moment for me. Life in America, as I saw it then, was so wondrous because I was unaware of anything negative about it. I never thought of the dangers that my father was thinking about as far as traveling through America as a Black man in an expensive car with an Asian woman in the passenger side who barely spoke English was concerned. I remember how the music and dancing on the trip made it so much fun. We listened to a lot of the Jacksons, and Michael Jackson's "Destiny" and "Off the Wall" albums are still some of my favorites. I also remember stopping in Baton Rouge to spend time with one of my father's friends in their lavish home with mirrors on every wall.

Arriving in New Mexico, we were met by the family of my father's friend and their daughter who was around my age. They helped us settle into our government quarters. At this time, I still did not speak any English so playing with other kids was difficult for them but not for me because I understood everything they were saying; I would simply reply in Japanese. I never felt strange about speaking Japanese to them because, in my world, that was normal. However, in their world, I was odd. One kid went so far as to ask my father, "Why does he understand everything, but we don't understand nothing he says?" My father replied that I spoke a foreign language. I wondered why my father didn't just say Japanese, but in noticing that his body language and expressions didn't show any hesitancy, I just moved on with it and the question never crossed my mind again. I didn't understand the cruelty of American kids toward those who are from other countries, because in Japan being a bully or just cruel to your peers can result in your ostracism. I adjusted to American culture so much that the father of one of the kids whom I played with came to my father to ask if he could tell me not to bully his son. I was surprised that this kid thought that I was bullying him. It was probably because I mimicked karate moves that I learned in Japan after school when I played with him. A few days after that encounter with the kid's father, I ran my bike into a window of a house and the doctor who removed the glass out of my eye was none other than that same father. As my father explained it to me, soon after the bike accident, I just started to speak English fluently out of the blue.

I never encountered racism or prejudice as far as I can remember during my time in New Mexico and that could have been because I was living on a military base. However, I could see then in my mother's eyes that she did not enjoy America as much as she did Japan, so she mostly stayed at home. This was probably due to a combination of homesickness and the difficulty in grasping the American way of life. After a year of living in New Mexico, it was now time for us to move back to Okinawa. I can remember my parents' joy as they prepared to return to Japan. My father loved Japan. He felt free there and its different culture expanded his mind in ways that he didn't experience in America as a Black man. We never had to have the "talk" in which he explained to me what life would be like for me as a Black kid. I never even thought to ask the question, nor did it cross my mind. I enjoyed every moment of life up to that time.

When we arrived in Okinawa, I can remember Ka-Chan coming up to me and asking if I had done my best while I was gone. "Do your best" in Japanese is *Ganbatte*, and it was always the first and last thing Ka-Chan would say to me. In America, my grandmother would always say to me "I love you", but in Japan one referred to effort more than emotions. I would always reply that I had, and I believed it in my spirit, which gave me a lot of confidence as a kid. My father allowed me to make a lot of decisions about my life as a child and would tell me to accept the consequences, good or bad. He never disciplined me physically because he didn't have to: in Japanese culture to let your family down was a shame more damaging than physical punishment.

Once we returned to Japan, I could see that friction was developing between my parents. My mother was absent more and it was mostly my father and I at home. I was now, at the age of six, on my own a lot. Every morning my father ironed my uniform for Christ the King International School. Christ the King was a K-12 institution, most of whose students were Filipino. There were also a few Japanese students in the school, but only three Black kids, including myself. I would wake up, get dressed, eat my cereal, and then proceed to walk to school, which was about two miles away from where we lived. This was a daily adventure to me. When I got home, I would have around four hours by myself before my father returned home from base. We lived in an Okinawan neighborhood that was far away from where my classmates and other Americans lived. It was there that I met Kuniyaki and Shinobu, who became my childhood friends. They were like a year older than me and attended Japanese school. My first encounter with Kuniyaki was a confrontational one. At the time,

Michael Jackson was my idol, and I had a *Jet* magazine with him on the cover. I was excited to show it to Kuniyaki but, instead of looking at the magazine, he beat me up on the spot. I cried and went home and told my mother what happened. She went outside to talk with him, but I could tell from her body language that either I was going to hide or face reality and confront my fears. Once I went back outside, I saw the respect that Kuniyaki had for me, and realized later that the beating was a kind of initiation.

Around 1982 my mother decided to leave us, and this would change my outlook on life: I began to rebel. It was like she just disappeared; I had no idea where she was living or working. My father looked at me in my eyes and said, "It's only you and I now, son." Before my parents officially divorced, I chose to stay with my father because I felt betrayed by my mother for having left without me. It was only when I was 40 years old that I realized her reason for having left: she didn't want to return to America. My mother never saw America as a land of opportunity, but rather as the colonizer that stripped her nation of its culture.

Every weekend I would stay at my grandmother's or my uncles' homes, and although not knowing where my mother was living or whom she was with never bothered me at the time, forgiveness for her apparent betrayal was something I did not even consider because she had made her choice in my mind.

Two years after my mother left, she arrived intoxicated at the house at around 3 a.m., banging on the door. My father went to open the door and I hid around the hallway. I can remember my mother pleading to come back and my father replying that too much time had passed and that we had learned to live without her. While she sat on the couch crying, she was holding a sake bottle that was about two feet tall. As she was beginning to raise it to her lips, it slipped out of her hand and shattered on the floor. At that point, my father told her that it was time to go, and she left again. The next weekend Ka-Chan and my mother arrived at the house to discuss the divorce and I can remember the question of whom I would live with came up. My father said to them, "Let Randy decide where he wants to go." Without hesitation I chose my father, a decision that sealed off any feelings I had for my mother. I chose to let her go because, as my father said, I had learned to live without her. However, being a motherless child had an enormous effect on me. Without anyone to nurture or comfort me, I grew colder and trusted fewer, but it made me love harder.

This was the beginning of my rebelliousness. I never disrespected my father, but I started to take more risks on the streets of Okinawa in my unsupervised time. My friends' parents didn't help matters. Shinobu's mother was a woman who ran a bar, so alcohol, cigarettes, women, and disorderly men were always around. Kuniyaki's father was a commercial real estate broker who associated with the Kyokuryu-kai, a clan that engaged in criminal activities. The men whom his father associated with had the traditional tattoos that identified their ties to the underworld. Of course, I didn't know this as a child but when my mother explained to Ka-Chan who my friends were she warned me not to get into any trouble with them and that she was going to have a conversation with my grand-uncle Ojisan about the situation. Ojisan was my grandfather's brother, who stepped in and became the man of the household to honor the Shimoji name when grandfather fell into alcoholism and began neglecting his family. Ojisan despised Americans because a Military Police (MP) shot him as a child when he was trying to get food for his family. It took him years before he would tell my father the story.

Listening to these conversations between Ka-Chan and Ojisan made me ask Shinobu if the stories about Kuniyaki's father were true, and he replied, "Why do you think Kuniyaki has all the nice stuff?" Kuniyaki's brother Taki was a muscular fellow who was always in his judo uniform and with his entourage after school who demanded respect from the younger guys. My eyes were beginning to open into a whole different world. I went from being an innocent and adventurous child to a wannabe teenager way before my time. My father did the best he could to shield me from the horrors of what he experienced in life, but the American colonization of Japanese culture even in Okinawa was something that he was powerless to protect me from. The colonial program of stripping conquered people of their land and culture to implement the conquerors' political and economic plans is destructive.

This was the beginning of my street lessons, and schoolwork was far from my mind. I was interested in the adventures we were going to have every day, like fighting, smoking cigarettes, stealing, and drinking. I remember one instance when we didn't have any money and decided to steal ice cream and candy from a local store while distracting the elderly owners.

I couldn't wait to get out of school because that was when my real education would begin. I would either fight or do any challenge that the older kids would suggest just to prove that I was part of their group. In Japan, I would always have to prove that I was part Japanese, just as I would have to prove my Blackness in the US. Fighting was something that I felt I had to do in order to be part of something. I never fought out of anger. I always wanted to love more than fight, but I knew that fighting was the way of proving my belonging to my male counterparts. Most of the time I would win by taking the extreme measures of using objects, such as boards or bats. I never liked to fight fairly and that's how I gained the reputation of being someone who would do anything to win. But deep down, I hated the feeling of hurting someone else.

Learning the street life in Okinawa filled an emptiness that I felt at home despite my father's efforts to raise me to be a good kid. He didn't imagine that my mind was ready for answers to important questions and, due to the respect for one's elders that is taught in Japanese families, it wasn't yet time for me to question adult decisions. Living with my father was a daily struggle not because he was a bad parent, but because he didn't realize that the freedom that he wanted me to have was causing me to grow up very quickly. This situation only further ignited my confusion and rebelliousness toward my family.

As the years went by my grades in school started to fall. I was more focused on mischief after school than on the idea of *Ganbatte*, which Ka-Chan would continue to say to me, but without the same hope in her voice. I was the first grandchild in my Shimoji family, but with four cousins who were full Japanese, the attention was beginning to shift away from me. I loved my cousins like they were my siblings, but I could hear in adult discussions about the future that they didn't include me in the family. When I asked my uncle about it, he told me that I was legally a foreigner. At that moment I felt displaced, which was a feeling that I had never experienced before. The more different I felt, the more rebellious I became. And because I didn't talk much with my father, I had to process my feelings by myself.

2
Holes in the heart

I was born at Stanford Hospital the day after Thanksgiving in 1971. The news about my heart was announced in December, a few days after Dr Greene requested a chest x-ray at my two-week-old checkup.

The pediatric cardiologist leaned against the table and said, "Sarah will need open-heart surgery", and my mom's vision went black. D-E-A-T-H thrust itself forward in bright white 3-D.

The doctor reassured my parents: I wouldn't die. I'd be fine. There was a big hole called an atrial septal defect, or ASD, but they knew how to fix it, which they'd do when the heart was grown, at around four years old. Dr Greene explained that they'd need to shut down my heart while they did it. That, my mom says, is what scared her. Of course, it would.

In 1976, I stayed at Stanford Hospital for ten days. They split my skin, sawed through my sternum, and stitched my heart whole. There was pain, of course—flesh pinched and burned, and chest bone broken open, and the daily shots and blood draws—but I mostly remember the pleasure. I clung to the praise I got for my extreme strength and bravery; for my emotional self-control while my body was anesthetized and sliced.

In my unreliable memory, it was later that same bicentennial year in the North Salem Baptist Church family cemetery near Savannah, Georgia when I first noticed the grave, a small old headstone overgrown by weeds in the corner that read: *Rachel Butler 1820–1901, Faithful Servant to George Adam Keller*. For a long time, I thought this early visit was when I realized that Mrs Butler had been a slave, not a servant, and thus began to learn more about my ancestors' history of enslavement on the plantations called Salem and Coldbrook that once surrounded the cemetery. The memory of becoming aware of this for the first time bleeds into the childhood memory of wet July heat, my skin slick against the red, white, and blue terrycloth dress, the knobby scar that runs from below my collar bone to the top of my abdomen still fresh, pulsing pink and tender. I know now that I am conflating the summer of the fresh rope scar and star-spangled dress in the family cemetery with later years, and probably with learning about the more complicated stories of Lucy and Steve. Seeing Mrs Butler's grave and translating "faithful servant" to "slave" must have been much later, when I was an older teen and curious enough to walk into corners and ask pointed questions, and not just of my mother, who hadn't known who Rachel Butler was until I started poking around. The conflation and confusion of emotions and dates makes sense, since what I learned in that cemetery was every bit as impactful to my life, every bit as traumatic and instructive, as my open-heart surgery.

I am a Californian. But every year of my life since I was born, I have visited Port Wentworth (once called Monteith and Meinhard for the two railway stations on that side of town) and Savannah, Georgia, where my mother, grandmother, great-grandmother, and great-great-grandmother, all named Harriet Keller (due in equal parts to tradition and first-cousin inbreeding), and their parents, grandparents, and great-grandparents Keller had grown up. Since the 1790s, Keller plantations—Salem, Coldbrook, Drakies—had lined the Savannah River and the rural inland of nearby Port Wentworth and Monteith directly along the path of Sherman's final March to the Sea. But although I'd met my distant cousins, who still lived on parts of that land, at shrimp boils and family reunions, and had seen old photographs of the buildings on Coldbrook in disrepair after the Civil War, what I knew of the South in my childhood was mostly my loving, progressive, public school-teaching grandparents who championed Jimmy Carter and were in frequent fellowship with Black folks at the Savannah Baptist Center. What I knew was being taken to that church and listening to hallelujahs and eating potluck suppers in the basement or at Shoney's Big Boy after worship, where my grandparents would invite all the servers to join hands with us and say grace. What I knew most—where we most often stayed—was the sea breeze and ocean water on Hilton Head Island, where my grandparents bought a small amount of land and started a Baptist Church in their family room, in 1959. I knew the salt on my face and sand in my suit from swimming all day, and then sweating in the cinder block beach house a few rows back with no AC.

I knew my grandparents, who lived in a small, pistachio-green tract house on East 58th Street on the outskirts of Savannah, loved me deeply. But I didn't really understand how much land had once been owned by my ancestors, or how many human beings had been enslaved by them, or what kind of trauma and shame we all carried, until I started asking questions much later.

I didn't know enough about the native Gullah Geechee people, descendants of enslaved people on Hilton Head Island, who were losing their land, acre by acre, to white developers as I swam and sweat and ate. And I certainly didn't know enough about the Yamacraw or Creek Native Americans of Savannah or the way my ancestors contributed to the retribution against and ultimate forced removal of the Creeks from Georgia, which began in the 1790s and culminated in the Trail of Tears in 1838.

Having bought land in Savannah, or on Hilton Head Island, doesn't make my grandmother a bad person any more than it makes me a bad person for buying a home in California on land that was once Indigenous, lived on and tended to by the Ramaytush Ohlone people before they were removed. However, it does make the places I call home more conflicted for me, now that I know. It means questioning who owns what and why. It means asking really tough questions and hearing the answers. It means telling the truth. It means reckoning with whiteness.

I must have been eight or nine when my mom started telling me about Lucy and Steve in the cemetery. Lucy Wheatfall and Steve Gillerson are buried to the side of the center of the cemetery, close to my great-great-grandparents, who lived at Drakies, a former rice plantation that then produced vegetables and potatoes after the war. Lucy's and Steve's headstones are relatively new, but small, and they say they were faithful servants too. I knew, based on the dates, that they hadn't been enslaved. I also knew, based on what I was told, that they may have been cared for, but they hadn't been free.

"I loved Lucy", my mom would say with tenderness and regret in her voice. "Grandma loved Lucy. We loved Steve too." And then, each year, she would repeat parts of their stories to me and give me snippets of her own.

Lucy and Steve lived with the Keller family in the main farmhouse at Drakies as domestic servants. They each had a room in the house, down the hall from Mommee, as my mom called her great grandmother, and her great grandfather. They used the same facilities and ate at the same kitchen table as the Kellers, but my mom doesn't remember them eating at the table together with her family, except when feeding her alone. Steve did most of the cooking, and Lucy most of the looking after the children and cleaning, and both were constant companions to my relatives.

"When Mommee came out into the fields from the house, Steve came with her", she told me. "Maybe to just make sure she was okay." She doesn't remember Steve working in the fields. I have photographs of my mother as a toddler on Steve's shoulders out on the farm, and the other Keller women leaning against him. I have photos of Lucy as a teen, casually crouched side by side with Mommee in the garden planting seeds and holding my grandmother as a baby in her arms. All of them appear at ease, even at play. But I know that Lucy and Steve were always at work.

Steve and Lucy were not related to one another, that we know of, nor do we know any of their kin. The story goes that Lucy's mother couldn't take care of her, so she was given or sold to Mommee's parents. I have no idea what part of that is true. Lucy is then described by family members as having been "given" to

Mommee as a wedding gift when she moved to Drakies from her family's plantation in Macon, Georgia.

It took me a while to question the math after I heard this story. Lucy was born after the war. Both Steve and Lucy remained "a beloved part of the family" throughout my own mother's childhood and early adulthood. So how was she "given", how did Steve end up as a lifelong servant, and why were they "kept"? Neither Steve nor Lucy ever married, had children, lived on their own, owned their own land or property, or were paid.

When I asked these questions, my mother said she supposed that Lucy and Steve worked as indentured servants to the family even after the war, because "there was likely minimal infrastructure to educate or help them, despite being technically 'free'". She also presumed that Mommee and Grand believed they *were* paying Lucy and Steve, or at least participating in a mutually consensual and beneficial relationship, in the sense that they were giving them food, shelter, medical care, and in some sense, a "family". I know that this happened often, that it may have been the best situation available to Lucy and Steve, and that it was not good enough. It was a situation that gave them no power or autonomy or opportunity for either.

"You know," my mother would say fondly and without fail at the cemetery, "I spent a lot of time with Lucy when Mother got sick."

Multiple times during my mom's childhood, my grandmother had declined into a semi-comatose state. My mom remembers the time her fourth-grade teacher took her home from school, then handed her off to a relative for a month, because my grandmother had been committed and my grandfather needed to care for her. My mom also remembers the time in high school when she came home to find my grandfather sitting with my grandmother, who stared off into the distance, at the kitchen table.

"Mother needs to go for a rest", her daddy told her, and then the ambulance came. During these times, my grandmother was hospitalized in Savannah and treated for depression and schizophrenia with electroshock therapy and chlorpromazine. Her mother, my great-grandmother Bobbie, had also been hospitalized for the same treatment at the infamous Milledgeville Asylum, where their version of electroshock therapy had been dubbed "the Georgia cocktail" and the eugenics movement had been popular. When her mother was "away", my mom would go stay at cousin Bettie's dairy farm in Port Wentworth, or at Mommee's vegetable farm down the road at Drakies, and bask in the care that Lucy and Steve, and other relatives, could give her.

My grandmother expressed often that she had loved Lucy since birth and told my mom that she had "tried to teach Lucy to read" and "encouraged her to navigate the world" on her own but had learned that all of that "came too little too late". Knowing the rate at which my grandmother gave money away to those in need, I am sure she also tried to pay Lucy, but found that she had no bank account, no social engagements, no place to spend the money or life outside my family's care. I don't know why no one set a bank account up for her. My grandmother died before my mom or I were wise enough to know how to ask her, but we both believe that the contradiction my grandmother felt in loving Lucy but recognizing the way society regarded her and also the way Lucy and Steve lived—both loved and respected and also dehumanized by lifelong unpaid service—within her own family both drove her career and life choices and also contributed to her depression.

My grandmother was a public-school special education teacher who eventually taught and served countless African American families and children (when the Black schools were shut down and thousands of Black teachers fired across the South, a tragedy of highly unequal integration that has left our school system with a dearth of Black teachers). But for years, while my mother was a child, Savannah was segregated, and my grandmother taught and worshipped only with children who were white.

My grandmother worked full time, as did all the women my mother remembers in their circle, an unusual enough fact in the 1950s and 1960s South, and I know her breakdowns did not happen only in the summer. I have no idea how she was able to cover her classes, but I do know that madness seemed to flow so freely through white Savannah society that it was accepted without stigma, a fact I find fascinating and telling. My mom remembers feeling no shame or noticeable repercussions whatsoever from complete disclosure about hospitalizations and schizophrenic breaks.

Family members often call the madness that runs through my ancestry "the Keller curse" and chalk it up to genetics and inbreeding. It is true that my grandmother's parents were first cousins, and that there are other related cousin couples in the line that I can count (not to mention the marriage of an aunt and half-nephew). It is also true that I don't discount genetics or epigenetics where mental illness is concerned. And my mom and I are sure that the cognitive dissonance of my grandmother's experience in the Jim Crow South did as much as anything to break her heart and drive her mad. How many other hearts did it break, and minds did it make mad? The only way to escape with an open heart and remain sane in such a system is if you remain unaware.

My mom insists that as a young person in segregated Savannah, she was unaware that anything was "wrong". She says she knew only love for Lucy and Steve, and warm personal relationships with other Black people as paid maids, caregivers, or in other service jobs. Her experience was that they lived and served, and that everyone seemed happy and well-treated. Her parents always spoke with respect and admiration for Black people, especially the Black schoolteachers they admired from afar. With very few exceptions, the people she knew did not fly Confederate flags or speak in overtly racist ways. It simply did not occur to her to question why Black people never ate in restaurants with her, went to the doctors she went to, played in the same parks, or swam in the same pools, used the same bathrooms, or went to the same schools. She does say that she was very aware that churches were segregated and assumed that was because Black churches were culturally different—louder, longer, full of gospel singing— with women deaconesses in white outfits speaking different languages. If anything, her impression was they were better. She can also claim the self-interest and ignorance of youth.

At 16 years old she left Savannah for undergraduate school at Blue Mountain, an all-women, all-white, Southern Baptist college tucked a short drive away from the University of Mississippi. In my mother's sophomore year, on September 30, 1962, she heard the helicopters racing over the Blue Mountain campus toward the "Battle of Oxford" as James Meredith, a Black Air Force veteran, attempted to enroll "Ole Miss" 45 miles away. She had no idea who James Meredith was or that this event was happening, and she quickly dismissed the helicopters until two days later, when she picked up a French newspaper at the Blue Mountain library. This, a French newspaper, was how she learned about the mob of angry whites who assaulted US marshals with bricks and bullets, killing two bystanders and injuring 206 marshals and soldiers before federal troops arrived (thus the helicopters) to quell the violence. She heard nothing of this news on campus from her professors or friends and does not remember discussing it with any of her professors or classmates, or her parents, after she learned about it. To this day, I cannot imagine how my well-intentioned grandparents and my now very "woke" mother lived together in the same household during segregation or reunited during holidays without any of these discussions arising and I certainly cannot imagine a college campus that is silent about race. She remembers such little open discussion or conflict about racial issues in her world to that date, and such complete submersion in what appeared to be an acceptable society to all those she knew, that she was blissfully ignorant of the intent and harm of the segregated caste system she and her entire family and their "faithful servants" lived within until she got to Indiana University (IU), was taught by a Black professor whom she chose as her advisor and mentor, and quickly realized that not all Black people lived to serve. From afar, she cheered on the integration efforts her parents were supportive of and impacted by as Black children began to attend their public schools back in Savannah, without realizing the harm that was happening to the Black schoolteachers.

My mom insisted that the combination of being at IU and meeting my dad, a Westerner who seemed to ooze a Swiss-like (and actually Swiss; his grandparents had come from Bern) sense of intellectual rigor, timeliness, and neutrality, had been what made her aware of the horrors of the Jim Crow South, as if my dad had come to Indiana with a multicultural past bursting forth or had instructed her. While it is true that my dad spent a junior year of college abroad studying at Hyderabad University in India, where he would have been witness to that unique caste system, when asked today, my dad remembers that in his elementary, junior high, and high schools in Seattle, there were no Black students (and only one Black teacher). At my dad's undergraduate school, Whitworth College in Spokane, which is only 2 per cent Black in 2023, my guess is that it was de facto 0 per cent Black in the 1950s, just like Blue Mountain was de jure 0 per cent Black in the 1960s. In my dad's army unit after college, where he trained in military intelligence before returning to his first graduate program, all his "Special Agent" colleagues were white (though there was a Black photographer on staff). He didn't have any real contact with Black people until he and my mom moved to the Washington DC area after IU. Just as my mom hadn't thought much about segregation growing up, my dad had been ignorant about the pervasiveness of white supremacist laws and lending practices throughout the nation that kept Seattle segregated, too.

In 1977, when I entered elementary school in progressive north-ern California, my mom expected, of course, that the school would be integrated. By the end of my kindergarten year, she had scheduled a meeting with the school principal.

"Where are the Black kids?" she asked him. She'd noticed one.

"Oh," he said. "They just don't live here."

3
Ancestral land

In 1987 my father and I packed to move back to Savannah where I had to stay a year with my family until my father finished his last year in the Air Force before retirement. We arrived at the airport and caught the taxi to Monteith. I can remember the smell of the air, which was very foul, and I asked my father jokingly, "What is that smell?" and he said, "It's the smell of home." I began to see the woodland area and thought to myself, "What is this place?" I was used to the city and now I was heading into deep backcountry where I had never lived before. Plus, now that I was going into my teenage years, living in the country didn't seem like an adventure anymore, just my reality.

There were no streetlights for about two miles. The only lights that were visible were those coming from the homes deep in the woods. This all looked like some horror movie to me, and I was beginning to hate the place. We pulled up to my grandparents' house, which stands on a 36-acre property, where my aunts also had their houses, and where my father would build his own after his tour in Korea. Getting out of the cab I could hear my grandfather yell out, "Who dat over yanduh?" I had no idea what that meant or what language he was speaking. My father replied, "It's me, Roy!" While I was unloading our luggage from the trunk of the cab, I was still thinking about what he said. Conversations between my father and I were always minimal; we didn't have long discussions or share emotions. He seemed so serious to me that I never wanted to disturb him with my thoughts, so I kept them to myself, and I tried to figure things out on my own. As my grandmother approached the edge of the patio, I can remember her saying, "O my Lawd, look at my chillum!" with gold dentures. I can remember the shine from her teeth. I never thought anything much of my father's gold tooth until I saw my grandmother's row of gold teeth and my grandfather's gold tooth, like my father's. I thought to myself that this must be a family tradition. As we walked up the stairs of Jim Walters' home, which seemed like an island on stilts, I saw my father's excitement in being with his family.

The next morning as we woke up to eat breakfast, my grandparents sat at the table with their Bibles and prayed over the food. After we ate, my grandmother handed me a Bible to read the chapters that she and my grandfather were reading. This was the first time in my life that I had to engage seriously with Christianity. Although I went to a Catholic school, I did so for the academics, and I didn't have to engage in the religious activities of the school. This engagement with religious rituals and events was all new to me, as was the way the preacher delivered his sermons on Sunday. It all seemed so theatrical, along with individuals dancing and fainting while rejoicing.

The dynamics of my relationship with my father meant that he did not share a lot with me about the world I was now in, which was the Deep South. As my father departed for his next duty, I was now in the hands of my family about whose morals, beliefs, expectations, and way of life I hadn't a clue. My first tragic moment came after my second day of middle school when I was sent home with a form that asked for my racial or ethnic identity. In Japan this was never required: either you were Japanese or a foreigner. I never had to identify myself as a color nor did anyone else. In Japan, we identified people by their nationality. When I asked my grandmother for guidance on what I should put down she told me, "If your dad is Black, then you are Black!" without explanation. Suddenly, I had assumed a Black identity instead of a national one. This changed my outlook even more and made me feel distant from my family in Japan, who did not include me anymore. This outcome also made me feel resentful of my father.

I struggled to fit in my first year as a sixth grader. I felt like an outsider in a place that was completely foreign to me. I missed Okinawa, my family, and my friends. I felt completely alone now back in America, much as my mother felt when she was here. I was so nervous because I didn't know anybody, and my cousins were in high school. Every morning I was left to catch the bus by myself while my cousins would drive to school. I remember asking them for a ride and they said no because they didn't want to babysit me. They told me that I would be fine, but I knew that I wasn't. This made me resent my family even more. As the oldest grandchild in my Japanese family, I was taught to look after my younger cousins no matter what, even if it came to feeding, changing diapers, or playing with them. So to come to the US and receive this sort of treatment from my own family was very foreign to me and left me looking for comfort elsewhere. I never feared anything but being neglected. That was my only fear.

Returning home from school was another world to me. I would get off the bus and go in the house, where my grandmother would always have snacks for us: cookies or peanut butter sandwiches with Kool-Aid. Those were my favorites. Then, it was time to do the chores. I usually helped my grandfather around the property with building shacks, fixing fences, landscaping, or other kinds of hard, manual labor. My grandfather always stayed busy on the property, which kept him strong into his mid-60s. I have never seen a man with his capabilities, not even in my father. He had hands that were as tough as alligator skin and he could lift a railroad tie on his own, which honestly scared the shit out of me. During the summer, we would also add landscaping the cemetery in North Salem, where the Keller family has a plot, to our chores.

As time went by, I made two friends at school: Jason Small, a Black kid, and Jason Culpepper, who was white. While Jason Culpepper and I always competed over grades, Jason Small and I competed in sports. In school I wasn't seen as a local, but as a kid from another country. Whereas Black people teased me a lot about being Asian, white people were more curious about what Japan was like and asked me questions about it. At this point, I didn't understand why even my own family never asked me about Japan or was not more curious about my background.

As I approached the gymnasium for Career Day with the rest of the sixth graders, I was in line between both Jasons. As we got closer to the bleachers, I started to see how segregation operated, with Black students moving to one area and whites to another. The teachers did not divide us by race, but the students did. Jason Culpepper assumed that I would follow him because

I was behind him but Jason Small, who was behind me, said to me, "Randy, come with us, we have candy", and what kid would refuse candy? At the end of the presentation, I started to make my way to Jason Culpepper to ask him about our next assignment and he said to me, "I thought you were different", and walked away. At that moment, I made another choice for myself and that was that I would identify with Black people, although I didn't understand the deeper meaning of that decision at the time.

After that experience, my grades started to slip, and I had to repeat sixth grade. This wasn't due to my lack of understanding of what I was being taught, but to my lack of effort. Now, all I wanted to do was to fit in with other Black kids. I did this by clowning around in class and constantly seeking attention.

My cousin "Tip" was already out of school, and he lived on the family property. His mother and my father were close siblings in the family, which made it easier to look up to him. He was also a military brat like me, and had moved around like me, so we had a certain connection. And he took the time to talk with me. He was the coolest guy I had ever known besides my father. Tip became my role model, or Big Brother in my imagination. Later, I figured out that he was a drug dealer, and I knew then what I wanted to be.

4
The Keller curse

In September of 1980, I started fourth grade with silver caps on my two front teeth and hints of a new self-loathing. The two were unrelated. I was the opposite of ashamed of my oral hardware, and happy enough, thanks to my comfort level with medical procedures, to have a physical injury to focus on. I remember the thrill of diversion, from the undefinable shame I was beginning to sense inside, to the fixable pain of cracking my mouth against the diving board. Also, I loved the nitrous oxide trips during my many dental procedures, and I had always admired the big kids' braces: I liked the bling of the shine.

By November, when California's governor, Ronald Reagan, replaced Georgia's Jimmy Carter as president, an event deeply mourned by my parents and grandparents, I had new white veneers for front teeth, and the distraction of the injury, as well as any blissful ignorance of my childhood, was over.

It started as a light shoulder tapping one night when I was ten, a vague feeling of worthlessness and potential loss of control over my own body. Quickly it turned into a heavy pressing down, and I became convinced that only vigilance would keep me, and everyone else, from discovering that I was the worst person alive.

I was riding my neighbor Tony's BMX bike by myself in the dusk in Concord, California, doing circles on the quiet asphalt, anticipating my favorite meal of pan-fried hamburgers and salad, and I heard things outside my head, like the bicycle chain squeak and the call and response of the Alaskan Husky named Sasha and the Golden Retriever named Henry barking back and forth across the suburban street from their respective backyards. And I remember the shape of the inquiry that appeared suddenly in my head, because it was a call and response too, and it came down upon me, *from* me, two-sided and with unwanted pursuit as I rounded the cul-de-sac corner, like an investigator trailing me in the near-dark as I tried to pump my legs away from it and pop wheelies.

Hey, it asked. *What if you're bad?*

What? I was stunned, pedaled harder. *No, be quiet.* I was polite even to myself then. My mom did not allow us to say "shut up" or use put-downs of any kind. We were always to be nice.

Do you know how you're bad?

I'm not bad. I'm good! I am this bike and this road and these legs that are good at soccer and Jeff-who-I-want-to-kiss-on-the-playground's crush and my new purple culottes I will wear Monday and this meal I will love and my parents who love me and I am normal: I am good and okay.

And then, *But what if you're bad?*

My parents seemed to believe I was all good and no bad. My mom often told me I was healthy and smart and athletic and nice—*I could do anything I put my mind to!*—and my careful, composed dad didn't disagree. These claims didn't feel like untruths or forced, and I was privileged to hear them as a child—they certainly weren't unkind—but after that night on my bike, they would begin to feel increasingly misfired and empty.

I skidded into my driveway, dismounted for dinner, and tried to calm the new race in my heart. *What if my whole life's a lie? What if I'm not good but bad?*

I spun my head around as if maybe I'd been caught, as if maybe someone had witnessed the weak moment, while I was humping Tony's bike toward Mom's hamburgers, when it occurred to me that I could potentially be rotten, in some way not normal, inside. I believed instantly it was one or the other: good or bad. I didn't know why. I didn't know how normal it was for me to fluctuate between nuances of self-love and self-hate as I came of age. I didn't know about all the cultural conditioning to feel "superior" or "in control" that I carried in my body because it was white, or the conflicting conditioning that I was inherently not as worthy because I was female, and that I would be downright bad or worthless if I wasn't smart, athletic, pretty, and straight. I didn't know why I felt evil in church every Sunday, why the concept of my humanity through the grace of Christ felt offensive to me, or why it all made me feel like I wanted to run away fast or else put my dukes up and fight.

I believed nothing anyone had done to me or would do for me had anything to do with it, and that my parents certainly couldn't help me. My parents were stalwart and good, and I knew they loved me unconditionally. But to be loved unconditionally by my parents and still feel disgust for myself felt like the worst kind of selfishness and shame. How awful, I thought, that they had gotten me.

Years of testing and numbing and yearning for absolute control over my "goodness" wired my brain in certain ways. Now I see the ways in which the onset of puberty and self-awareness in a culture that prizes heteronormativity and perfectionism would have been plenty to knock a deep-thinking little girl off her rocker. Add the role of individual brain chemistry and genetics, and some of us are more susceptible to emotional sensitivities than others. And what role might epigenetics have played in this?

The latest epigenetics shows that emotional trauma can be passed down through multiple generations through changes to the epigenome, a swirl of biological factors that affect how genes are expressed. My mother seemed to have been skipped over by the "the Keller curse" but I had always felt—since the first time I saw Rachel Butler's grave—as though I carried the trauma of white supremacy in my DNA in a particular way.

In 1983 I started middle school one block up the street from our house. Oak Grove Intermediate was known as "a bad school" by some fearful parents, thanks to the fact that it bused in students from one or two "bad" areas of Concord, already the ugly stepchild to the shopping mecca of Walnut Creek. But everyone in my neighborhood went to Oak Grove, and there was never a question of whether I would. My mom worked in a majority Spanish-speaking elementary school in one of those "bad" areas, and she knew the naysaying parents' objections were thinly veiled racist hogwash. She was also, by this point in her public-school teaching life, abjectly opposed to private schools. In our world, only rich people who felt that the perfectly good public schools weren't good enough for them went to private schools. My mom felt that my brother and I would find a way to thrive wherever we went, that public schools did not necessarily produce lesser students, and probably did produce better citizens. She was both correct about her assumptions and privileged to be able to have them about our particular schools. We didn't know what it was like to go to public school in places where institutions were dangerously lacking in funding and support, or from families where additional educational support was not an available opportunity at home, or with skin that wasn't white. My mom had every reason to trust in the system, or at least trust that the system was meant for me, and even more for my brother, and for people like us with parents like her. It *was* good for us. But were private schools better for some people? Who got to choose, and why did some people have choices while others did not? She was right that the fear about Oak Grove for me was hogwash. I got a perfectly good education there.

The summer before I started high school, my mom, Rick, and I went to Savannah and Hilton Head without my dad for the first time. This wasn't explained to us. We were used to our dad coming with us, but then, we also easily accepted him not coming. At the time this seemed natural, like nothing to ask about. Now, when I think of my own children, I am astounded by it.

There were reports of chickens dying from the heat on the day the three of us drove out to visit a distant cousin named Luke, a hog farmer about my mother's age who lived in rural Georgia. Luke was on his second marriage to a spunky dark-haired woman named Gineen who endeared herself to all of us with her close-ness to her mother-in-law, Doris. Gineen drove Doris around in her red Corvette and planned trips around the world for the two of them. It was fun to watch them have fun together. They could afford this because Luke was also the only family member who had parlayed farming into the kind of wealth that bought him hundreds of acres, sports cars, and a beautiful modern home. Everyone else I was related to lived in old, modest houses.

Luke told Rick and me that we were going for a ride.

"Are we going far?" I asked Luke.

"Naw."

"Your house is big!" Rick said.

"We got all this space," Luke nodded. He turned, chest puffed up, to my ten-year-old brother and said, "not on toppa one another like in California." As far as I knew, Luke had never been to California. I scoffed at him under my breath, and then he said with a chuckle: "You know, out here, you got a problem with your wife, ain't nobody got to know." Rick and I shared a look, and a red flag flew in my chest. Luke threw a six pack of Budweiser in the truck.

We bumped along already-made wheel tracks through the woods until he stopped near a clearing, and we all got out of the truck. Luke leaned against it, lifted his chin, and said: "This where the niggers buy their beer."

He'd stopped across a dirt road from a dilapidated convenience store, where two Black men had just emerged and were walking the opposite way just out of ear shot, or at least I hoped they were. I don't know what my face was doing but I remember being stunned and feeling like I'd just been hit.

"I know y'all call 'em colored," Luke continued. "but they always be niggers to us."

In my memory of that day, I muttered: "We don't call people colored either, you fuck." But my memory fools me. I don't think I said anything or did anything other than jump back in the truck to get us moving. I remember catching Rick's eye as we drove back to the farm and baring my teeth. He looked as disturbed as I felt. When we pulled up to the house, we both told our mom we wanted to *go*.

In the car on the way out we told my mom the story, now having processed it a little. She was horrified, as she always was by hateful behavior, but not as surprised that Luke was openly racist as I'd hoped. I'd never heard any other family member say openly racist or hateful things. If anything, my grandparents did an awkward form of the opposite. "Don't ya know," I heard my grandmother say once with a big celebratory smile on her face, "a doctor moved in down the street, and she's *Black*!"

"Wonderful, wonderful", my grandfather would have earnestly agreed and opined.

"Terrible", my mom said, about Luke. "We won't go back."

"Well, that's the South!" my brother said with disgust.

"Don't be fooled", my mom told us, as she had before. "These attitudes are everywhere. Just more out in the open here."

"Stop defending it!" I said.

"It's pretty bad", Rick said.

"I'm not defending Luke," my mom said, her eyes still on the road, making space between us and that farm, "or his racism. I'm saying it's in California too."

My mom was used to defending her homeland halfheartedly. She knew its brutality as well as its beauty. She loved Savannah, and also felt constricted and conflicted there. But I assumed she defended the South out of the kind of innate defensiveness one often feels for their home; one based in nostalgia, not reality. It turns out she knew something we didn't: that white supremacy, like misogyny, was everywhere in America. It just looked different and manifested in different ways. I didn't yet know the ways in which it had manifested itself in me.

That summer, after we returned to California, a Black man named Timothy Lee was found hanging from a noose at the Concord BART (Bay Area Rapid Transit) station a few miles from our house. It was ruled a suicide, though there had been a racial attack on two Black men by men wearing white robes a few hours before Lee died, and just a few miles away. Seven months after the first questionable lynching, an unnamed Black woman was found hanging from a tree near a bank parking lot, about ten miles away from the Concord BART station.

In our home we weren't allowed to gossip or say hateful things about people at all. There was never any racial or sexual slur. We couldn't even say "shut up" to one another. *No put downs* was the biggest rule. Before that fall, I don't remember noticing anyone speak hatefully about non-white people in California. But I began to hear the words "faggot" and "chink" and "sand nigger" and "Spic".

I heard these words from other kids, often kids who identified as the slurs they used, and always passed off as lighthearted jokes, never spoken as harshly as Luke had, but still there, by which I mean still just as harmful. I began to understand they'd been there all along. I just hadn't heard them.

"You were right", I said to my mom. "It's in California." She nodded.

What I didn't say was anything to my friends, especially my Black friends—not Aaron, not Julie who played goalie on my soccer team, not Dani a fellow freshman at school—about what had happened near the BART station or what happened in casual conversation, day to day. I don't remember any of us talking about it, ever. There was a small minority of Black kids at our school. How did they feel about being outnumbered? Were they scared by the lynchings? Did they even hear about them? I only knew because my mom told me. Were they offended by the jokes? Did they hear the same jokes I did?

Before the danger of social media and texting and words that lived forever online, we wrote notes to each other on paper. Now, we romanticize them as silly and harmless. But in 2019 I found one from an older boy I'd temporarily liked in high school. "Look," he wrote for no apparent reason in the middle of the note, "I'm talking like a nigger! Ain't tha funny?" I don't remember what I did about this—if I called the boy out on it or not—or if I even read the whole note and fully registered it. Most likely I just shoved the note in a box and tried to forget, thinking I'd eventually toss it. But I kept them all. They are mostly earnest offerings of love and support. Some of them though, have become proof of inherited hate.

One night during the fall of my freshman year, our family of four had dinner together as usual—sitting in the same seats—Rick across from my mom, and my dad across from me. As always, there was a classical music record on low, and the TV was off, and we ate slowly and discussed our days as we listened to each other, just like the studies—not yet conducted—now recommend.

After we'd eaten, my mom said: "We love you both very much, but your dad and I have decided to get a divorce."

My dad didn't say a word. I suspect he couldn't. He bowed his head and brought his white cotton handkerchief to his eyes. We'd given it to him, Rick and I, for Christmas.

"Can I go to Tommy's now?" Rick asked.

"Yes, be home in an hour." My mom understood his desperation to escape. I sat there a bit longer, watching my dad try to lower the handkerchief, breathe, and raise it again, but Rick's anxious exit marked the last time we all four sat at the dinner table together.

My dad slept in the den for a bit, then he made a quick and easy move a few blocks away to an apartment, which never stopped feeling exotic to me, like a faraway hotel room, even though it was walking distance from school and from home. Rick and I visited him for dinner, which always included salad with his home-made salad dressing, two nights a week. I didn't consciously feel as if there was anything I'd lost, any sort of stability and safety I was desperately trying to steal back into my life.

That year, my friends and I shoplifted almost weekly. We visited the two-story mall with hundreds of stores covering 79 sprawling acres, including a gargantuan dilapidated Macy's and a McDonalds. The stealing just sort of happened, as if it was an inevitable reaction, like scratching an itch. We three blonde 13-year-olds lifted tiny, sweet plastic tchotchkes: summery white Hello Kitty key chains and ice cream cone erasers made by big companies too far away to matter (to us), the occasional root beer-scented pencil, and once, a bag of Jelly Bellies. In the mall we became overconfident soldiers, swaggering through dime store aisles pocketing all that stuff we didn't want or need, except that I needed to take it.

Then we moved on to clothing and got caught. The team of two security guards, a white man and woman in plain clothes, quietly followed us across the threshold from Macy's into what had seemed a second earlier to be the safety of the inner sanctum of the mall.

"Come with us, please", the man said, and we spun around to see their badges. One of my friends, the least involved, immediately started sobbing. The other was the one who had lifted the overalls, which were for me. I remember the terror of knowing I was busted, and the safety of knowing nothing *that bad* would happen. The team brought us to the surveillance room, a dark chamber filled with black and white security screens, PA system levers, and buttons that I remember as if it were a windowless cockpit. They used a few light scare tactics, loosely mentioning the police and "misdemeanor" as well as jail time before they told us they were *sure* this was our first offense and explained that they'd be banning us from all Macy's stores for a year and calling our parents to come collect us.

"You girls are lucky", the woman said. "This could have been worse." I knew she was right. I never seriously considered that we would be arrested, but I felt relieved that the police wouldn't be involved, and I felt some relief in being caught, because it gave my self-loathing a name. Although I couldn't have articulated it at the time, I had been exchanging the fear and self-loathing that felt infinite—*Am I good or am I bad*—for the common bad behavior of teenaged shoplifting. I was glad my mom was about to get a call about some overalls my friend tried to steal, not about the existential crisis in my heart. While I knew it would be painful to witness my mom's severe disappointment and shock, I knew it would be fairly easy to convince her, truthfully, that I would never do anything like that again.

That was kind of the end of my illicit life, other than activism later. I drank and smoked pot in high school, but not a lot, and I didn't really go to parties. I never saw anyone using other drugs, or out of control, and I never felt unsafe at any point, or witnessed violence outside of athletics. The black eyes I sustained were from head collisions in soccer matches. Concord was 20 miles away from Oakland, which was being decimated by a crack cocaine epidemic that my friends and I heard about vaguely but could not have understood. Most of us rarely saw the news or paid attention to it, beyond what they showed on MTV. Where crack was concerned, I heard only Reagan's "Just Say No" campaign and vague jokes about "crack heads" until we began to hear lyrics referencing the epidemic, starting with N.W.A.'s "Dopeman" in 1988. Later, I learned most of what I knew about what was happening in the Oakland crack epidemic from Too $hort in "The Ghetto" in 1990. What I knew wasn't much, and that information came through music that served as entertainment to us suburban kids. I see now that listening to it in my flavor of teenaged angst and feeling a vague proximity to it by sharing the same 510 area code lent me what felt like license to identify with "the hard life", which now feels like shameful appropriation.

We never saw cousin Luke again. He and Gineen got divorced shortly after my parents did, and in 1986 or 1987, Gineen and Doris took a trip to San Francisco. I remember Gineen's bright red nails shining like rubies along with her smile while we ate crab and sourdough bread at Fisherman's Wharf. She seemed truly happy to be with me, and I liked her. The next summer, when we were back east, Gineen drove to Savannah to meet us for lunch, and after lunch she climbed in our car to go get dessert on River Street. We were on our way back to her car when Gineen looked out the window, saw a teenager, and said: "Now what's that nigger doing on *this* street?"

"No", my mother said immediately. "We don't use that word."

"Aw shoot", Gineen said. "Sorry y'all", as if she'd simply let a regular swear word slip. Rick and I sat stunned in the back seat. My mom had simplified the issue to language, but we all knew how loaded it was. We knew the dehumanization and hate that was beneath. We dropped her off at her car and said goodbye forever.

5
Black in America

It was in eighth grade that I had my first experience with crime. A lot of my friends lived in the Fellwood Projects and most of them were already selling crack. To be able to sell drugs with them in the projects, I joined the basketball team, which gave me an excuse to not go directly home after school. By this time my father had returned from Korea and built a home on the family property. With my father's financial security, there wasn't anything that he couldn't give me. But the identity crisis that I was going through over being Black without an explanation of the meaning of Blackness, like how the meaning of being Japanese was taught to me in Japan, left me to define Blackness by what I saw daily and that was selling drugs. My family would often tell me that there were things we weren't supposed to talk about or that I asked too many questions when I wanted to know why things were the way that they were. These unanswered questions made me feel very isolated.

Despite the challenges, I quickly adapted to life in Savannah. I attended a predominantly Black high school, which gave me a deeper understanding of Black culture in America. I learned about the struggles and triumphs of Black people throughout history and gained a newfound respect for their resilience and strength. At the same time, I also faced discrimination because of my mixed heritage. As a half-Black and half-Japanese teenager, I faced discrimination and prejudice from both sides of the racial divide. Some people were confused by my identity, and I was often asked insensitive questions about my appearance and culture. One of the most significant challenges I faced was trying to fit in and to make friends. Before my father left for Korea, he built a basketball hoop for me on the property, which gave me an outlet and focus when I was alone. I quickly became good enough to compete against the neighborhood and school kids and to join the middle school team. This gave me a sense of belonging. I used basketball to gain acceptance and going to a predominantly Black school meant that most of my teammates came from drug-infested neighborhoods and half of them were already dealing. This fascinated me because it was like the lifestyle that I had in Okinawa, but with drugs.

But the streets of Savannah were more dangerous than those in Okinawa. Moving to Savannah during the crack epidemic was a challenging time. The crack epidemic had devastated many Black communities across America, and Savannah was no exception. The city had seen a rise in crime and poverty, and it was not uncommon to see people struggling with addiction and homelessness. For me, it was no longer about drinking beer, smoking, fighting, or stealing from stores. Now it was about the politics of the streets: what you said, how you said it, and whom you said it to. My life would be on the line by taking chances with the law and the streets.

Where it all started for me in the drug dealing business was when my older cousin, who was a drug trafficker, took me on runs and had me count the money for him, which could be as high as five figures. The adrenaline of the moment gave me a sense of excitement and made me want to do this. While my cousin and I rode around the city making pick-ups, I would imagine myself as the guy next in charge, although I was only in the eighth grade at that time. I had friends in school who were already dealing but they were dealing for another reason: survival. But for me, it was an adventure and a way of finding and embracing my new identity as a young Black man in America.

During basketball practice (I made the varsity starting team as a freshman) one day, one of my teammates, Quinton, brought in a shoebox full of crack cocaine, which was about a quarter kilo, and asked me to join him in selling it after practice. At the time I worked at a drive-thru fast-food restaurant, which was a perfect place to sell from. The manager had a crack habit herself and didn't mind me selling from the restaurant and would warn me of any possible police busts, as long as she got a cut of the profits. At first, learning the difference between rock sizes was the hardest part of selling. My consciousness of knowing that I was doing wrong always haunted my mind, but my rebellion against my father and his family gave me the fuel to continue making money and to come up with an exit plan to be on my own. Still, I felt very conflicted when thinking about my Japanese family, but I knew that I would never return there to live.

For a few months this arrangement was going well, but then Quinton's uncle was arrested for distribution, which ended our supply. At the time, I was living in a rural area that was seven miles from Savannah, and I didn't have the means to go there daily to resupply. As a result, I asked my cousin who was a trafficker to supply me, and his reaction both surprised and angered me. He responded, "You know if Uncle Roy finds out, he will kill me!" and refused to sell to me. I felt that he was being hypocritical considering that he was the one who introduced me to this life, but deep down I understood that it wasn't my father he feared but the guilt he would feel if something in fact happened to me. I continued to work after school and play ball, but the importance of an education beyond just getting a job was not instilled in me by my family. I was never taught that the more education you have, the more opportunities you have of landing a lucrative job.

As the summer of 1992 approached, my father sent me to Japan to visit my family, which I was very excited to do. My father and my grandfather drove me to Atlanta airport and told me to come back with a changed mind. Neither of them knew what mental damage had already been done to me by being Black in America. Landing in Okinawa, my family welcomed me in with a joy that I missed. They saw the little boy who had left a few years back, but what they couldn't see was the young Black man that I had become while I was gone. Although I understood my native tongue, at first it was very hard for me to translate my thoughts from English to Japanese. Later, I would learn that speaking different languages is not about the languages themselves, but the personality and culture that go along with each language. It took me around two to three weeks to stop mixing English into my Japanese sentences. During my time in Okinawa, I did not see my mother often as she was either in the Miyako Islands, where our family is from, or in bed all day after working in the bars at night. This was very painful to me, but I learned to cope with my pain by ignoring it and fueling it with anger.

I often went to visit my childhood friends Kunyaki and Shinobu when I had time off from working with my uncles at their construction site. My job was mostly to lend a helping hand like an apprentice: bringing all the tools to the site and carrying all the materials needed to build the interior of the home. My uncles were great carpenters, and my summer job instilled in me a work ethic that would help me in the future. Getting paid was an enjoyable moment for me because the whole crew would show up to my uncle's house and have dinner, drinks, and talk shit until his wife would bring out the envelopes and bow to thank the entire crew for their efforts. After receiving my envelope, I would go and visit Kuniyaki and Shinobu, who were still in high school but had motorcycle licenses and formed their own motorcycle gang, or *Bosozoku* in Japanese. This subculture of young rebels without a cause started in the 1950s. This subculture was also the beginning stage for most guys who wanted to become *Yakuza* members or just troublemakers, both of whom were called *chimpira*. Being called a *chimpira* was a disgrace to your family. To be initiated into the *Yakuza* usually required that someone in your family go to the office of the organization and request your admission into the family. I watched many of my childhood friends who were without fathers or mothers be accepted into that organization and be looked down upon by Japanese society.

During my summer in Japan, I experienced working with my family and enjoyed my time with my friends. My family knew that I had changed but didn't mention it because they knew that

I would be heading back to Georgia and they wanted to enjoy my presence. What I didn't hear often anymore was Ka-Chan telling me to do my best; her words of encouragement were slowly disappearing. I would go out at night and come back two or three days later, and she would ask me if I had been in my old neighborhood when she smelled alcohol and cigarettes on me. She would then say that I was shaming the family, which really angered me because she had no idea of what I had gone through in America. While feeling this anger, I couldn't wait to return to Georgia because now I understood that I wasn't accepted in my homeland anymore. I had lost the sense of belonging without being able to explain what I was experiencing psychologically and emotionally. My whole summer was filled with learning my uncles' work ethic and the street ethic of the *Bosozoku* and the *chimpira* world of extorting local shops, selling stolen goods, and getting into fights.

My Japanese friends never treated me as an outsider or as a Black man. They were fascinated by my stories of the American crime world and would often talk about connecting with me in America to further their criminal careers. They also used my knowledge of English to solicit soldiers and their families to sell alcohol or meth, which was commonly used by soldiers and foreigners because the punishment for Japanese citizens who trafficked in drugs was harsh. Personally, I never handled the drugs but translated for my friends and earned money that way. Kuniyaki was never involved in dealing as he was more into school, working on motorcycles, and just being the brains of everything. Shinobu was more hands on and a partygoer, so I hung out with him most of the time.

When it came time for me to return to Georgia, I was sad, but I also missed my father. Plus, I wanted to leave a country that I didn't identify with anymore. I felt like I wanted to be the stereotype of an American gangster, but what I didn't realize was how much I was distancing myself from my Japanese family in the process. Returning to Georgia, I can remember my father picking me up and asking how everyone was and if I learned anything, but I couldn't tell him the truth because I was still so angry inside. I was looking forward to my family asking me something about Japan, but no one did; it was all like I had never left. Our discussions went right back to church, as if church was going to save me from the situation I was in.

In the tenth grade in 1993, I was more advanced in my criminal mind than I was a year prior. But dealing drugs for me was never so much about the money as it was about feeling free and alive. That's what gave me the thrill. It was the fear of the unknown and of not allowing fear to defeat me like it did when I believed that being Black was to be fearful and weak. My thinking then was about how I could instill fear into others without considering the consequences of my actions. Thinking like this was what made me feel free mentally and emotionally, but the constant message of being an endangered species, as the media hyped the deaths of young Black males in the 1990s, was always in the back of my mind. I never imagined living past 25 years old; I always thought I would end up either in jail or dead. My family never really gave me any hope outside of serving God here on earth and of being delivered to a heaven of eternal happiness when we pass away. All the music and movies that I was drawn to at the time all had negative messages for me as a Black man. There were few, if any, influences besides religion to become something positive in my community. I always understood that there was a higher power, but the debates over whose interpretation of the higher power was the correct version just didn't sit right with me.

Back in school, I returned to my normal routines of finding ways to be away from home, where every conversation was about religion. Being on the school basketball team was my escape. My coach would often tell me that I had talent but mentally I was too angry and resentful. With my grades declining and knowing that I would have to repeat the tenth grade, my father decided to send me back to Okinawa to become a Japanese citizen and stay in Japan. But what he didn't realize was that it was not going to be an easy task for me or my family in Okinawa.

After riding in the car with my father on our way to Atlanta airport in silence for almost three hours, he finally said to me in a serious tone, "Randy, I don't want to bury you here in America, but you are acting out here like a nigger, and I never taught you that! I always taught you to be Randy! Not a Black man, Negro, or a nigger! You have lost yourself and you learned to be a follower, and I believe the best place for you to be is back with your mother in Okinawa." I knew he was right deep down, but my rebelliousness wouldn't allow me to admit it because I still blamed him for leaving me alone with my Black family without preparing me for the drastic change of cultures. He gave me a long lecture but at that age there was no way he was going to get through to me to undo the damage that had already been done. Boarding the flight and looking back, I was going to miss my father and it hurt. Arriving in Okinawa, my family had no idea what was going on in the States, but I told my mother that I wanted to stay and either get a visa or change my citizenship. My family knew this would be a hard task and it wasn't something that they wanted to pursue.

While working with my uncles in the construction business, my old habits of hanging out with my friends began to resurface and anger my family. I knew that they would send me back to my father but now I was seeing things as a Black man. I recognized the differences in how they treated me and my cousins who were full-blooded Japanese. There were plenty of moments when I felt alone and angry about my feelings instead of understanding them. I was the oldest grandchild in my Japanese family, but any time the subject of legacy was discussed, I was missing from the conversation. When I would ask why I was not mentioned, the answer always was "American". At the time, I took that answer as one that disrespected me and my Blackness. I knew then that I would return to Georgia despite my father's wishes.

I stayed in Okinawa until the end of October, which meant that I missed the registration deadline at my high school. I decided, then, to stay with my cousin who lived in the Yamacraw Village housing project and pursue drug dealing full time. Against my cousin's advice, I did what I thought at the time was how to be "Black" in America. I wasn't brought up in a culture of Blackness so, by the time I reached Georgia at the age of 13, I had my own interpretation of what being Black was from my peers and from whatever hip hop culture showed me in lyrics and videos. I am not saying this to blame hip hop for my or anyone else's choices, but unless you were born and raised in a system of oppression there is no way you can understand how hip hop shaped my youth and ideas about Blackness. You can only have an opinion about it and that's all. As a young adult you often think you are immortal. So my attitude was why not live life to its fullest, regardless of the outcome.

My first week in the projects was all a learning experience about the struggles of the people who lived there. Everything was a hustle; you never knew what was really going on unless you were totally engaged in the street life. When I took my first thousand dollars that I made in Okinawa and bought an ounce of crack, I immediately stood out on the stoop. My cousin's next-door neighbor, Rob, yelled out to me to come over. He remembered me from playing basketball in high school and he asked me if I was Tim's cousin. I nodded and he said, "I remember you from Groves High School and the hamburger joint!" I started to get curious about him and let my guard down a little bit. He instructed me not to stand on the corner near where my cousin's house was because you never want the cops to know exactly where you live. As Rob and I got 22 oz cans of Budweiser and started talking, he took a liking to me. He gave me advice and started to teach me the ropes of drug dealing. Since I started with a large amount of drugs as a corner boy, he wanted me to be his customer. From the amount of product he sold me, I could usually double or triple my profits. How much money I was left with depended on whether I chose to spend my earnings or save them to climb up the ladder. One piece of advice that I can remember Rob giving me was "to roll with flavor. You got to roll with some flavor!" By that he meant that I should associate with other players who were established in the game already. I had to build my reputation by engaging in robberies and stick ups, and ending my need to flash and stay out all night and morning hustling.

This life took a toll on my relationship with my cousin Tim, whom I lived with. After five months, he decided to take me back to my father's house. Driving to my father's house I felt shame and guilt. I wanted to continue with the life that I was leading, but since I was still a minor, I had no choice. I stayed with my father until I was 18 years old and went to the Richard Arnold Alternative School to earn my GED. But my rebellious ways were still there because my father still never explained to me what it took to be a Black man in America, a lesson that I had to learn on my own. I got a job as soon as I turned 18 at a sugar refinery, saved my money, and moved to a trailer park.

Within two days at the trailer park, the television set that my father had given me and that I had in my room for over ten years was stolen out of my camper. That TV was the only thing that reminded me of Okinawa and now it was gone. Slowly my memories of Okinawa were fading. The residents of the trailer park were mostly white, which meant that I would have to be especially cautious if I was going to sell crack there because of the potential of police informants. This is when I met Dave, who was a Vietnam vet. He was an alcoholic but a resourceful individual who knew just about everybody around town. I enjoyed getting Dave a 12-pack of Natural Light beers and listening to his war stories and reflections on life. He had a great deal of wisdom. As I sat on his stairs that went up to his trailer, I asked him about the possibility of making some money by selling crack for me. He replied with a "Sure, as long as you take care of me. My

VA check will cover the rent and bills, but I need money for my habits." I replied, "Sure, Dave." I needed Dave to make the hand-to-hand transaction to remove me from direct sales because there was a big difference in punishment between intent to distribute and possession. So, once the agreement was made, I started saving my money from work so that I could visit Rob in Yamacraw Village for a package. After a month, I went to visit Rob, but since I hadn't seen him for close to a year, I didn't know that his status had changed due to numerous police raids and setbacks. He was now a low-level dealer like me. That's the nature of the business, so I learned. While evaluating my own journey, I now understood how fast things can change in life.

I always understood that I was different from everyone else in my Black community. I was always asked what I am "mixed with". That question always made me feel like an outsider. And when I answered that my mother is Japanese, I would hear anti-Asian racial slurs from Black people. So where do I truly belong, I would ask myself. I was doing everything in my power to assimilate into my Black community, but I was not fully accepted into it, much like how I was not fully accepted into the Japanese community. The Japanese culture in me was always trying to emerge but the thought of my grandmother telling me that I was Black made me think that I could not be both Black and Japanese. This division built a lot of anger, sadness, and confusion within me that made me self-destructive. The racism that I experienced from my two communities forced me to think a lot about what it means to be Black. The limited answers to this question in an oppressive society explain why most young Black males define success by either playing professional sports, rapping, or getting involved in drug sales.

Years went by with me going back and forth between working and selling dope to make a living for myself. One day I was in such a bad place after having lost my product in police raids that I went to the unemployment office and signed up for Job Corps. Job Corps is a residential career training program for low-income at-risk youths who are between 16 and 24 years old. I applied as a homeless 19-year-old, and I was accepted into the Earle C. Clements Job Corps Center in Morganfield, Kentucky. This was my first time that I traveled anywhere in the States as an adult, so I was kind of excited to start something new. I didn't know any-one else who had attended Job Corps, so I had no idea what was in store for me besides being trained in a trade and receiving my technical certificate. The Department of Labor office gave me a Greyhound bus ticket and a bus schedule. I was told that I needed to be on the bus that I selected, or I would lose the opportunity. I carried my passport, birth certificate, and the few clothes I had. I left the rest of my belongings with a friend. As I looked out the window of the bus, I realized just how big America really is and started to doubt that I would ever return to my father or to my family in Okinawa.

The Earle C. Clements Job Corps Center sits on approximately 700 acres of land, with approximately 90 buildings. It was here that Abraham Lincoln gave his only political speech in the Bluegrass State. The Center is contracted to house 1,022 students, with 14 dormitories for residential students. While in processing, Job Corps issues you camouflage fatigues, boots, a pair of running shoes, and physical activity clothes as if you were in the military. But what I soon noticed was that participants were creating their own designs by cutting the fatigues or drawing on them. I also noticed that the majority of people in Job Corps were Black, with a few Hispanic and whites. These young people were mostly juvenile delinquents, orphans, or kids from the Caribbean who separated themselves into gangs according to where they came from. I would eventually fit in with the Georgia and Florida crew.

I was fortunate to be in the 500 block, which housed the student government body and the academically strong participants. Most of the Georgia and Florida crew were in the 300 or 400 blocks, which were close to a half a mile from each other. What I experienced at Job Corps was not an educational system, but a criminal one. Drugs and gang culture was a big part of this institution, and most of the administrators were in on this racket. Each student got paid around $60 bi-weekly and some kids had money sent from home, so the flow of cash within the school was a big problem. I witnessed stabbings and fights between the gangs. These scenes would further solidify my negative image of my people because I did not see anything positive about being Black. And about those Black people who were successful, I learned to consider them either Uncle Toms or bougie. I did not understand that my feelings about them were based on other Black people's envy of successful Black people.

In all of this I met the president of the Job Corps' youth, who was at least 6 ft 6 in tall and weighed about 300-plus pounds. He took a liking to me and told me that I was different, but that the way that I was conducting myself as the number two guy in the Georgia and Florida crew was beneath me. He also told me that he would get me a job at the snack bar after classes that paid minimum wage. This snack bar was run by the son of the mayor of Morganfield, and he thought that this would keep me out of trouble. In my position at the snack bar, I oversaw the work of about 70 employees and the sales of at least $15,000 bi-weekly on commissary goods and drugs. The guy who took me under his wing was a guy we called "Ace". Ace was from Lakeland, Florida, and was about 5 ft 9 in of pure muscle. He had dark skin and dreads, which made him look like the epitome of a 1990s Florida boy. Ace and I came on the same bus together to the Center, but he was already familiar with the situation because his brothers had spent time here before.

After our orientation we met back up in the chow hall. After we had eaten, he said to me, "Let's take a walk. I want you to meet the guys we need to clique up with." As we walked, I could see the different gangs all around the 500 block, which was very different from how people acted in my area. Here, I saw people loitering, high on drugs, people dancing, and heard music blasting. As we approached the leader of the crew, whose name was Cruz, a half-Cuban and half-Black guy, Ace introduced me to him and, as I reached out my hand, Ace swung at Cruz with two combination hooks that knocked Cruz out. As Ace stood over Cruz, he yelled out, "Look here Niggas! Me and Goldie run this now and if you have a problem let me know!" As he said this, he kicked Cruz in the face for everyone to see. When I saw this happen, I knew that I was now a part of this system and labeled in a way that I wasn't prepared for, but there was no backing out of it now. I knew that I would have to be on guard against those people who would defend Cruz and against campus security. I never thought of questioning Ace on his actions because he was my guy, and I decided to stick with him no matter what for as long as we were in Job Corps.

I started my vocational training as an auto body specialist, and I loved it because I always had an interest in cars. But I used my class training to operate in my position in the gang and, after class was over, I would go to work at the snack bar. Steve, who was the son of the mayor of Morganfield, was involved in trafficking marijuana into the Center. After a month, Steve learned of my position in the gang and approached me with the idea of supplying us. I looked at this as a great opportunity to keep our drug sales discreet. As Ace controlled the guys, I was able to control the way our clique made money through the sale of marijuana and commissary goods.

Our operation lasted for about six months until a riot broke out and Ace and I were brought in for questioning along with all the other leaders of the gang. Since Ace was frequently involved in violent outbreaks, the Center expelled him. I was able to stay because there was not enough evidence against me and no one to implicate me in the actual riot. I was alone now and just focused on working with Steve, who was glad that, with Ace gone, I would be loyal only to him. About a month after the riot, Sheila, who was from Miami, introduced me to a young lady named Pam. Pam told me that she wanted to make money and we agreed that we would meet near her electronics class where I could give her some product. I skipped class to make this happen and discovered that she had set me up. Campus security suddenly drove up to me and asked me where I had the marijuana and I told them that I had thrown it under a table in class and that one of the other students picked it up. While I was searching for the bag, the security officers became impatient and told me to get in the car and escorted me to the administration office, where I was interrogated for information about my supplier and where I had stashed the money. During the process I learned that Pam was their informant and that I was being expelled from the program. I was never allowed back to the dorms, and I was instructed to wait for the next Greyhound bus. Curiously, my release paperwork stated that I had completed the auto body repair course, but there was no mention of the reason for my expulsion. My money was seized, and I was put on a bus to Lenoir, North Carolina, where my girlfriend from Job Corps went after she had completed the program. Luckily, I had been sending her money on a weekly basis and we had enough to start a life there.

My girlfriend and her mother met me at the bus station, but as we drove to her mother's house, I realized that I was back in a low-income area where crime was the way of surviving. I stayed in Lenoir for about six months before I went back to Savannah and my familiar grounds in Yamacraw Village.

Rob, I would learn, was locked up at the time but some of the guys that I knew from around the way gave me a spot on the corner. This went on for about six months before I was right back to where I was before the Job Corps, but this time I was homeless. I had to migrate to the east side of Savannah so that my friends would not see me this way. I was on the streets for about a month, going from hotels to a shelter. As I laid in the shelter bed, I often wondered why I was putting myself in these situations. I also thought about my father and his dreams for me.

One day, after a few weeks in the shelter, I was sitting in Franklin Square in downtown Savannah facing the First African Baptist Church. I proceeded to enter the church and Reverend Tillman greeted me with such grace that I just humbly told him about my situation, and he invited me back to Bible study that evening. He also said that he would speak to the church elders about sending me to a retreat center in Atlanta that would help me get my life back in order. In the Bible study meeting, the women elders heard my story, felt my sincerity, and gathered around me to pray for me. They sent me to the retreat center the next day.

The retreat center looked like a plantation with old slave quarters and newly built outhouses for guests. I got out of the van and some staff members welcomed me with a prayer and walked me to the bunkhouse where I would live for the next eight weeks. This was a place where people who felt they were on the wrong track would come to change their lives. I was never a heavy drug user, so this was not my reason for entering the retreat center. My reason was to answer the question, "Who am I?" Daily chores, weekly Bible study, and church services were the norm at this retreat center. I met there a guy named Frank who was from New York and in his late 40s. I could tell that he was neither an addict nor gay, but an opportunist. Frank used the retreat as a getaway from whatever he was involved in and used the time to allow things to die down. Still, Frank was a good friend to me and taught me the power of observation.

Once you finish the program, you have a four-week stay in a half-way house at a church in Atlanta. That church assigns you a job either at the church or somewhere else. My assignment was to be a minister to the youth in the community. Fortunately, I knew the Bible fairly well because I used to go to almost every church service with my grandmother in my teenage years. When I was approached for this job, I was brought into the Reverend's office, and he suggested that I work with the youth group, where he believed I would have the greatest impact. He wanted me to encourage young people to attend church. I would be one of the youngest ministers in the organization as I was just 21. I had an uneasy feeling about this because I knew that I wasn't fully dedicated to serving God in that way, and I didn't believe I was worthy of being a minister and bringing the word to a congregation. When I asked the Reverend about how I could prepare to preach, he explained to me that I would have an assistant who would help write my sermons and that all I had to do was memorize and rehearse them before services. This didn't sit well with me so the next day I gave Frank a call and he invited me to his home in Buckhead. I told him all about the situation and Frank laughed and said to me, "All these religious groups are scams!" Then, he asked me whether I had a plan either to get away or stay and comply with the Reverend's terms.

Leaving that church was on my mind but at the same time I needed a place to stay and a way of making money. Frank suggested that I work with his girlfriend's brothers, Kaisaan and Isaam, who were part of a crew from New York that sold merchandise at concerts and games. The merchandise was all bootleg, and we had to conceal it under our baggy clothes inside the venues and then go aisle-to-aisle selling it. The catch was that if we got caught by a marshal, we would have to bail ourselves out and meet the team at the next venue in case we couldn't make it on time for the scheduled departure. Kaisaan and Isaam were both members of the Nation of Islam and were always trying to get me to convert to Islam. I never did but I still tried to act like them.

I was with this crew for about four months, and we made our way all the way to the Lincoln Projects in Harlem. This place was always busy, and I learned there how ruthless the streets can really be. Isaam always looked out for me. We would wake up at his mother's place and go to the print shop to make T-shirts and other merchandise for the next few events. He and Kaisaan took me to the Mosque Temple 7 twice, where I was asked to convert to Islam, but I refused. As time went on, I began to miss home and decided to head back to Savannah and Yamacraw Village. But this time I headed back with barely any money, so I needed a place to stay and a job.

Rob was now out of prison so he was back at his family's house, where he let me stay while I got myself together. Every night we shared our stories, and he would always tell me that there was something bigger waiting for us and that we just needed to do the right thing in the meantime. But he also understood that being Black in America meant that there were limited opportunities for us.

About three months passed by and then the police raided his family's house and arrested Rob. As this was his third strike, he would go to prison for a long time. His wife Ruby and I went to visit him in the county jail before his sentencing, and he asked me to look out for Ruby while she made the move to Hinesville, Georgia, and I agreed. Hinesville was an army town and later I would learn that this was the place where the Quartermans had been enslaved. Dealing in Hinesville was risky because most of my clientele and most of my transactions took place on army or federal grounds.

6
Fatherhood

It was in Hinesville where I met Trina and we began dating. We soon had our son, Taijon. As I held him, I began to reminisce about my father and where my life and Taijon's were headed. I began to cry and think about how I was fucking my life up and how I needed to change. Discussing my thoughts with Trina was a hard topic because she enjoyed the dealing lifestyle, and she didn't see any other way to live. I knew within myself that this was not where I wanted my family to be.

While I was still hustling in Hinesville, Trina's house was raided because a guy who used to live at her address prior to her moving there was wanted by the Georgia Bureau of Investigation in connection with multiple murders in Walthourville, Georgia. These murders were connected to a turf war over trafficking cocaine from Florida to Georgia. I wasn't living with Trina at the time, but I heard about the raid, and I went to check up on her and Taijon.

Matt, a guy whom I would hustle with in Hinesville and who knew the brother-in-law of the guy who committed the murders, came up with the idea of finding the drugs that the murderer stole from the victims. We sniffed coke for about four days straight, scheming and searching for where the stash was hidden. On a rainy day we were outside a trailer park poking the ground with a soil probe, trying to hit any object that we could. Finally, we hit an object and dug up three popcorn tins full of cocaine and crack. This was the most drugs I had ever seen in my life, which scared the shit out of me because I knew people died over this. Once Matt and I divided the loot, I started hustling again and noticed that individuals whom I had never seen before started to come around. One guy asked me if I was Goldie and if I had some work for him. I glanced at him up and down and realized that he was armed. I knew then to deny who I was and that it was time for me, Trina, and Taijon to move. I asked her if was possible for us to move to South Carolina where she was from, and she agreed.

I stayed with Trina and Taijon in Trina's family's house for two weeks with few movements outside of it. I enjoyed playing with Taijon. We were in Summerville, South Carolina, where most of the people in the town were white. This was the first time that I had lived in a majority white environment. What I noticed was that most Blacks there were very submissive to whites, but I didn't see anything threatening in how the common white person treated Black people. How white cops treated Black people was a different matter altogether because I knew that Blacks were more subject to arrest than whites there.

I started working at a marble company, installing tubs and sinks. I liked the job, but I didn't like the fact that Black employees were never promoted to leadership positions and were always assistants to white employees. One day I rode with the nephew of the owner and asked why he picked me to work with him because usually I saw him alone. He was a young, brawly guy who I knew could lift sinks himself. He answered, "You're different. You are not like these niggers I know!" Deep down I was very offended by this because I knew what my father taught me about how even poor whites thought that they were better than Black people. I asked him, "Are your ancestors English? Did your family come from wealth when they arrived in America?" He replied, "No, my family is of Irish and German descent.""So," I said, "you're a nigger, too?" I saw his face get red and he asked me where I was from. I told him about my background, and he became very curious about my journey. He asked me if I spoke another language and I replied, "If I was born and raised in Japan, why wouldn't I speak Japanese? If my mother is Japanese, I should speak Japanese, right?" I could tell that he had never been spoken to before in this manner by someone Black, especially with his power and color. After that conversation, he made me his permanent assistant, which I didn't mind because now we had an understanding.

I never thought I would ever see racism in this form, but as I now started to take notice of how the company treated other Blacks who worked there, I couldn't stomach it and decided to quit. As I sat in a club one day afterwards, having a drink and sniffing cocaine, an individual in a uniform approached me, but it wasn't a police uniform. I asked him about it, and he replied, "I'm an army recruiter!" When I asked what he wanted, he answered, "I wanted to see if you're willing to sell me some snow?" I told him that what he saw in front of me was for my personal use, but that I could take his number and get back to him later. He sat down and, as we talked about his work, I gave him a bump. At some point in the conversation, the idea of joining the army ran through my head, although I had always said to myself that I would never join because my father had served, and I wanted to do something totally different from what he did. The recruiter asked if I could get clean. I told him, "Of course!" We then made a deal: in exchange for the rest of the cocaine that I had, he would arrange to get me into the army in a week. We both smiled and I met him the next day to sign all the paperwork. Then, I had to play the waiting game before I could go to the Military Entrance Processing Station (MEPS) in Columbia, South Carolina.

In my happiness, I went to tell Trina and Taijon about my decision and that I would finally be doing something positive in my life. As I told Trina how our lives would change, she said to me, "Goldie, why do you want to join the white man's army? They will never treat you like a man! You are always a drug dealer and that's what you should focus on!" This hurt me deeply, but I was determined to go forward. I asked my father to look in on Taijon any chance he had, because I knew that if I came back, it would destroy any possibilities of my redemption. In August of 2000, I got on a bus to Fort Leonard Wood, Missouri. My life was now on the right path, and I was going to find out what type of Black man I could be in America.

7
Privilege and protest

After high school graduation I worked as a waitress, slinging burgers and pie at Marie Calendar's, and I ran a lot. I wrote to the UCSB soccer coach to tell him I'd be trying out for the team. He told me when to show up, more than a month before school started, and gave me the summer training regimen. The work-outs were physically hard, five to ten or so miles a day of running plus hundreds of sit-ups and push-ups. They were especially hard before or after an eight-hour restaurant shift. They weren't mentally hard. Compared to intrusive thoughts, or as a distraction from intrusive thoughts, they were a relief. I liked the game of seeing how much I could hustle each shift in tips, and the immediate pay off for good service or likability. I liked running for my own sanity, and the challenge of seeing how I could train my body into exhaustion and shape. I restricted my intake to Raisin Nut Bran and spaghetti with marinara sauce, except when I succumbed to scarfing down slivers of pie while I was working. After I binged, I restricted more heavily. I took long baths at night to wash away the smell of grease. I was 17 at the start of August and ready to go off on my own. It wasn't a typical leaving.

One Friday afternoon I packed my cleats and a few things and caught a ride to Santa Maria that I'd organized with a man and his family I'd never met. He was a friend of some friend, none of whose names or faces I can recall. He agreed to let me stay at his house in Santa Maria all weekend, where I ate pasta and ran. On Monday morning, I caught a ride with the man to Santa Barbara, where he worked. He dropped me off at the deserted UCSB athletic field at 7:30 a.m. I sat there alone for an hour, admiring the fog hovering over the coastal pitch before folks started arriving. I had no idea where I would sleep that night, but I figured I could crash with someone on the team. My mom agreed to this arrangement because she assumed I'd be home in a week on the Greyhound. She was right that my odds of making the team were low, but she'd underestimated how singularly focused I'd been. I ran circles around those other girls. A kind sophomore from Colorado named Cari let me stay on the couch in her Isla Vista apartment, which she shared with a roommate.

"You're not really good enough", Coach told me a week later in his no-nonsense Brazilian tongue. I was the last one to have a meeting with him. One by one, each of the other walk-on hopefuls had emerged from the classroom and said they'd been released. "But…potential", he said to me. "I'm keeping you." I didn't care about his less than confident acceptance. The point had been to make the team. To be the only one to make it made it sweeter. The actual soccer playing was almost superfluous. I was starting to realize that success was also a distraction from fear. I felt high.

"You're breaking the flow, freshman!" Coach would yell at me during practice or warm up. I probably never would have gotten minutes even if I remained healthy. But I was half relieved to pull a hamstring early on and have my bench time called an injury. I spent more time in ice baths and with ultrasound machines that with a soccer ball.

I moved into the dorms mid-season and attended my first college course, which was Black Studies 60A: Blacks and Religion. I missed a good bit of that quarter, lucky to be half healthy and very lucky that the entire team, which was only 15 women large, got to travel. We bused up and down the west coast and flew to the east coast to play (in my case, sit), and nearly beat, University of North Carolina. I enjoyed the admiration I earned with my dormmates and family and friends back home, of being the only freshman on a nationally ranked team, without actually ever seeing the field to earn that admiration. The shame and self-loathing crept back. I felt that I was not as good as I got credit for being, because I wasn't. Could I still call it imposter syndrome if I really was an imposter? I knew I was well out of my league. I often found myself bingeing at the Hometown Buffets where the team stopped for dinner, or sitting in the back of the bus shoving Hostess cakes down my throat when Cari was asleep beside me. As soon as the season was done, I told Coach I wouldn't be coming back the following year. He was the kindest he'd ever been to me in that meeting. I suspect he was relieved.

Divorced from my team, I finally had a good bit of time to notice what else was going on around me on campus. It seemed like everywhere I looked, other students who looked like me were doing what was expected of them: living the best years of their life in paradise, carefree. There was sunshine nearly all day and stars shining bright over the ocean at night. There were also actual stars. Gwyneth Paltrow was in my friend's acting class. The juxtaposition of this glittering expectation and my self-loathing enhanced how I was feeling: lost and depressed. I was not enjoying going to parties on Del Playa or hanging out in my bikini, and doing these things made me feel like a different kind of imposter. But there were two places I did not feel like an inauthentic ass: at my job as a barista at the coffee cart on campus, and in my Black Studies class. I have no idea what my classmates and professor thought of me, but they were welcoming and kind, and engaged in authentic and serious debate. I was ravenous for it. I continued taking Black Studies courses, by far the best undergraduate or graduate courses I have ever taken, and I credit the Black Studies teaching community with inspiring me to find my community in deeper political discourse and action.

I declared political science as my major fairly quickly and began getting interested in student activism. I attended every speech I came across in the middle of campus at Storke Plaza, and I walked through the dark streets of Isla Vista, usually alive with keggers, holding a candle and chanting "Women Unite! Take Back the Night!" I was passionate about preventing violence against women even though I was only adjacently aware of violence against women and was privileged to have never felt unsafe. At that time, I couldn't have even imagined Elliot Roger's misogynist Isla Vista massacre in 2014.

Then, at the end of 1990, as the Gulf War loomed and inflated fears of a Vietnam-like conflict swirled about the country, I started attending antiwar meetings to learn about planned protests and about how to instruct students to help others avoid the draft. We were hope-filled and catastrophizing, and maybe a little bored.

On January 15, 1991, hundreds of us met in Storke Plaza to protest the impending beginning of the combat phase of Operation
Desert Storm. I probably couldn't identify Iraq from Kuwait from
Iran on a map if I'd been asked, and I didn't really understand foreign policy, either. I knew that Jeff, my first love, who had joined
the military after high school, was being deployed to Iraq, and
that made it real to me.

"No blood for oil!" we chanted as we marched to Cheadle Hall,
the administration building. I would like to think I meant anyone's blood, and it's true that I didn't want anyone to die. It's also
true, evidenced by the fact that I hadn't protested lots of other
atrocities happening around the world, that I meant American
blood, and namely Jeff's blood. I didn't recognize my ethnocen-
trism or ignorance at the time. I would have denied it with a claim
of staunch antiwar pacifism: another truth, but not the
whole truth.

There were 200 of us. We sat quietly in Cheadle Hall for hours
before the police came. We knew that protests were happening
on a larger scale on other California and US campuses, and in
many places around the world. We all agreed we wanted to be
arrested and that this was how we would make our statement
against the war.

It was dark when they handcuffed us in pairs and put us in the
paddy wagon. I didn't know the person I was handcuffed to.
I didn't know anyone else getting arrested that night. Someone
photographed each of us as we got in the bus. Later, we knew
the FBI had been involved, investigating some alleged pipe
bombs on campus, and we suspected it was them. We were

taken to the small county jail that night, and once we were all seated outside and ordered to stay silent, the armed officers began to walk around the perimeter and try to convince us to get up and sign ourselves out on our own recognizance before we were booked. Their motivation was likely quite simple: they wanted to go home.

"You don't really want to be arrested", one said, hovering above me. "Your leader is saying forget it. Just go home." This wasn't true, but we had no way to know that. "There are dykes in there, in the jail, you know", he growled at me. His assumption that this would rattle me, given how much thought I'd given to that particular fear already, made me chuckle and only made me more vigilant. Maybe 20 people left. I stayed. I was put into holding, then booked, and then I went back to my apartment. I went to class and work the next morning and night, as usual.

A protracted court case followed, thanks to UCSB's chancellor, Barbara Uehling, who insisted on pressing charges against a group of peaceful and politically engaged students. The other 180 students and I would be offered legal representation, then denied it, then offered it again multiple times. There was a time there when I believed I might not get representation at all and could possibly end up with an actual crime on my record. But this was not one of my fears, and I had no dreams of military intelligence security clearances. Eventually, I was "sentenced" to community service, spent a few months cleaning toilets at the preschool in Isla Vista, and the charges were dropped. In no way do I think I made a difference in the (very short) Gulf War, but I'm still proud of what I did. It was one of the few times in my young life that I could honestly do something "wrong" that I felt right about. I'm proud of the fact that I didn't ask my parents for help of any kind or try to wiggle out of the consequences of my actions. They had supported my actions, but I don't think they even knew I was sitting in court, juggling attorneys, or at any legal risk. I went through the process. It was relatively easy for me to do so.

I had a friend at UCSB who had a serious boyfriend, was on birth control, used condoms, and still accidentally got pregnant. Luckily, in California in the 1990s she had easy access to an abortion, but given the stigma against it and the shame she felt in having a basic health procedure that any person should be able to access, I began to think and read about the violence anti-abortion protesters and terrorists had wrought against even legal abortion providers and patients in the 1980s, and about the need to erase the stigma and shame associated with abortion. I finished my undergraduate coursework early. The intrusive thoughts came back. I don't even remember what they were about. I spent the last six months of my time at UCSB crying to my incredibly patient, longtime boyfriend, about my unexplained but seemingly bottomless angst and writing a 100-page thesis on the argument for legal abortion. I thought it was a philosophical study in history, not preparation for a post-Roe America.

After graduation, I knew only that I did not want to go on to law school. I had a Eurorail ticket for the entire three months of the summer, thanks to a graduation gift from my mom. I voyaged off on my own, moving around to different hostels whenever the mood struck, to Madrid, San Sebastian, Grenada, Interlaken, Bern, Lucerne, Berlin, Budapest, Prague, Paris, Amsterdam, Venice, and finally, for the last three sun- and meat-packed weeks, Thessaloniki.

I was running through cities, trying to escape myself. It didn't work, except as a grand experiment in self-reliance and living on $15 a day. I was mostly miserable, aware that I couldn't outrun my own skin, until I fell for a guy on my last stop in Greece, and almost stayed.

I moved back home and took a job as a receptionist for a telemarketing arm of a mortgage loan company. My former high school track coach, who had declared his love for me back in high school, was managing the telemarketing center, and I didn't have any better ideas. My mom had given me six months to live at home rent free, this job paid remarkably well, and I was eager to get out and into my own place before the six-month "pay rent now" deadline. I studied for and got my real estate license and then moved into a condo in Fremont with a kind, divorced dad of two and fellow mortgage loan agent named Lee. I wasn't good at selling loans or refinances (or anything but the evening's special), even during the early-1990s refinance extravaganza, so at night I also waited tables at El Torito. I went back to taking long baths to wash off the restaurant grease and soak my feet. This continued until the married CEO of the mortgage company drove me home from a boozy lunch one day and kissed me in his white BMW. I was happy to let him kiss me, and I kissed him back, but when I got out of the car, I somehow knew he'd never speak to me again, and I felt thoroughly used. I didn't necessarily feel out of my league. I just knew I wasn't in the right one.

I went back to soccer, sort of. Coaching an U7 AYSO (American Youth Soccer Organization) team relies on a heavy dose of clowning as well, since kids that age are not yet making their own decisions to be on the pitch. There was a girls' team in Palo Alto that needed a coach and I volunteered. The parents, who usually coach the AYSO teams, frequently a painful operation, loved me. I got immediate requests to babysit, then an offer to move into a pool house in Atherton in exchange for babysitting one family, and cash in exchange for babysitting another. I was happy there, feeling more than qualified for that level of soccer and using my spare time to write, but I knew I was not in a long-term profession. I knew I wanted to be able to support myself financially. It was 1994 and Silicon Valley was just starting to hit puberty. It was pretty clear that the technology industry was a huge opportunity, but what I really loved was academia, politics, and writing, and I had purposefully not taken a single math course in undergraduate school. I am forever indebted to all those Stanford alum soccer parents who suggested that I absolutely could pivot my focus and apply to Stanford for graduate school, in engineering. Someone suggested an engineering major called organizational behavior, which sounded a little bit like the politics of organizations and seemed just soft enough for me to bite. The alums suggested talking to professors—"just go over there, you pass by campus every day!"—and, having had great experiences with professors at UCSB, I did. I dropped by office hours, talked to various professors who were extremely encouraging to me, and applied.

8
Deployment

Once I arrived in Fort Leonard Wood, my basic training started with a three-day orientation, where we were sized for our uniforms and filled out administrative paperwork to start our processing into the US Army. It was a very relaxed three days, with medical and physical training every morning at 5:30 a.m. Most of the soldiers were not used to waking up that early but my life experiences prepared me for what was coming. At least, that's what I thought! After three days, we were loaded up in a cattle truck with our duffle bags to our chest. We had two duffle bags and our personal luggage, which, we were told, had to be a carry-on-size bag from home. As the truck started to pull off, the drill sergeants started to yell repeatedly at the top of their voices, "Put your face in the bag!" Now, I was beginning to get nervous and had no idea where I was headed. I tried to peek out, but I heard from the side of me, "You, shitbag! I said put your face in the bag!" I then mushed my face further into the bag. This continuous yelling lasted for the entire 20-minute ride, which had everyone either afraid or nervous. I could hear individuals now crying to go home but because I was familiar with this feeling from family and street situations, I understood that there was no reason to be fearful. Still, the fact that I couldn't see where I was going made me feel uneasy. Once the truck stopped, we were given instructions to get off the truck: "Now in a single file line exit the truck with all your belongings in an expeditious matter!" While they were saying this, I understood that I had to closely observe my surroundings and follow instructions so as not to get yelled at. I thought about my son plenty of nights when things settled down, but we were not able to send mail or call home until the third week.

Joining the army came naturally to me, maybe because I was a military brat and I saw my father serve for so many years. I called my son's mother after my four weeks of training to inform her of my status and plans for our future. She replied to me that she was not interested in that life and that I was denying what I was good at, which was being a dope dealer. Right then, I made the hard decision to not return to Georgia because I knew that it would cause me to fail again. Unfortunately, my son became the collateral damage of my decision. I later learned that these decisions are commonly made in Black communities because of the poverty in many of them. And how the person who is trying to do something positive in their life is frequently looked upon as a sell out or as someone who is trying to be white.

There were individuals in my basic training platoon who had never been around other races and these social adjustments were commonly addressed by our drill sergeants. However, when we had our personal time, we would spend time with people in our racial group. I imagine that this was because most people identify with people from their own culture and that it is with them that they feel most comfortable. I generally felt more comfortable alone. It wasn't that I denied my own Blackness, but I always wondered if I was Black enough to other Black people. And I didn't force myself to hang out with whites because of the resentment of white people that was instilled in me by my family. As graduation approached, we took a night infiltration course, which is a confidence-building training exercise where soldiers crawl 100 meters while live ammunition is fired over their heads and simulated explosions erupt on the ground around them. This was a scary situation, not because I had never been shot at before, but because the explosions made the simulation so real that your adrenaline runs very high. Basic training taught me how to become a team player and how to work together with others. I learned to embrace the culture and love it. There was nothing negative that the drill sergeants instilled in us.

After we graduated, we were sent to advanced individual training, where we would learn a specific skill to perform in the army. As the drill sergeants read everyone's orders, I was told to wait and later I was told to report to headquarters. I was nervous about why I wasn't assigned a skill or given orders to where I was going next. Once I reported to military personnel division, the staff member told me that I had signed up with an open contract and that I was to pick a job that was listed on his printout of courses. He suggested all the combat jobs, but being 25 years old and wanting a skill set, I knew that I wasn't going to receive that training in any combat job. I looked through the sheet and noticed the Quartermaster Corps, and as I asked the civilian about the job, the word "Supply" stood out to me since I knew about supplying as a street supplier. When I selected this MOS (Military Occupational Specialty) of 92Y, which is Unit Supply, I had found my calling within the Army.

My advanced training in Fort Lee was a little more relaxed than basic training but we still had drill instructors who guided us through physical training and classes. The first time I experienced true racism was in training when a white female soldier claimed that I had attempted to rape her in the break room of the instruction facility. She made the accusation at morning breakfast where most of us from basic training always ate together. One of the female soldiers in our platoon had told me that the woman who accused me and another female were fighting in the barracks the night before at the time that the alleged attack had taken place. While we were discussing this at the table, she passed by and I asked her if she had gotten her "ass whooped" the night before. The table laughed although it was not my intention to embarrass her but, from the multiple conversations that we had had, she knew how I was. She told me to "Fuck off!" and walked away. I didn't think anything of it, but at lunch the women in my platoon told me that they were questioned by the drill instructors whether they ever felt threatened or intimidated by me. This confused me, but I still thought nothing of it. Later that evening I was called to the office of the first sergeant, who was the unit drill sergeant's supervisor. I grabbed my battle buddy, who was required to be my gender and to go with me virtually everywhere. PFC Carradine, who was about my age and whom I had a lot in common with, was always my battle buddy and I was his.

As I sat at the conference table writing my sworn statement on where I had been and what I was doing at the time of this incident, it occurred to me that we were always closely monitored by the instructors during class and that no one was allowed in the break room during class period. Plus, considering the size of the room and that it had see-through glass, someone would have walked by and noticed if four individuals were in the break room. I wrote this in my statement, and I was quickly questioned by the commander about why I included this observation in the sworn statement. I replied, "because this is my statement, and this is totally a ridiculous accusation". I was told to shut up and be quiet, but I knew that my observation would rise through the higher ranks. An hour went by, and when I was called into the commander's office he told me that her accusations didn't have enough evidence to punish me, but he wanted to know about the incident when I was intoxicated in the club. Right then I knew that I would not leave his office without any punishment, so I agreed that I might need counseling. After my first session with the Army Substance Abuse Program the counselor cancelled my session because she understood that I didn't have an alcohol problem because I was intoxicated one time on a weekend. This infuriated me because I knew that what was really at issue was the fact that I was Black and the accuser was a white female. I looked at the Army differently after that incident. I was always angry toward authority, and the incident caused me to look for reasons to question or expose authority any chance that I had. After graduation in December 2000, I received orders to report to Fort Hood.

I flew into Killeen, Texas, which is the home of Fort Hood. I was nervous but I was more anxious about what the new adventure would be for me. I was assigned to a personnel service battalion that handled all of Fort Hood's records and my job was in staff headquarters. My supervisor assigned me the job of battalion armorer. This duty gave me a sense of responsibility and confidence in keeping weapons in service for soldiers who would need them for combat. Soldiers made up most of Killeen's population, but there was a darker side to Killeen where crime was as visible as it was in Hinesville, Georgia. What I learned as I stayed in Killeen was that prostitution, drugs, and stolen vehicles were very much part of the local culture off base. I knew some soldiers who were running drugs from Texas to other states and committing insurance scams, but I knew that I couldn't go down this road anymore.

I remember sitting in the dayroom of the headquarters on September 11, 2001 as we watched on TV the plane that crashed into the twin towers. Soldiers were approaching the commander to draw their weapons out of the armory, but the commander and I knew that we would wait on instructions before engaging in any act. I felt a sense of urgency to defend my country, and at this time all racism, classism, or individual prejudice went out the window. Our nation was under attack and our patriotic duty was more important at this moment than anything else. Once the initial impact passed and all security measures were taken on the base, our training escalated and intensified, and we all knew that it was time to deploy to Iraq. The only fear I had was of dying from biological weapons. I accepted the fact that I could get blown up, shot, or stabbed but I didn't want to die from breathing chemical weapons. As we prepared to deploy, I decided to ask my girlfriend to marry me. She is from the island of Samoa and although I had never heard of or met anyone from Samoa before I met her, I came to realize how similar their culture and appearance is to that of African Americans. We were in the same battalion and the first time I saw my wife was on a field where we would conduct our morning physical training. It was always dark in the morning, but when she walked by I used to see the vision of my mother, whom I hadn't seen or spoken to in ten years. My wife would always encourage me to contact my family, but since I was so distant from my Japanese heritage, I felt ashamed to do it.

As we trained and prepared for our deployment to Iraq, I was getting more anxious and nervous. I called my father to tell him that I was going to war, but he just replied with "be safe". I wanted to be comforted but I knew the situation that I had created for myself back home and I knew that I was alone, even if my wife was deploying with me. She was on a separate mission that required her to leave two weeks ahead of me. When we started to board the plane in formation with all our gear, I started to think more about what my life was worth. I sat next to my comrade, Kimbrough, who was at least 6 ft 2 in and 210 lbs of manly man from Louisiana. We had just started to reminisce about our lives back home when there was an announcement on the plane that a Scud missile siren had been activated on the flight line and that we needed to put on our nuclear biological suits (NBCs). While we were donning our gear there was another announcement asking if anyone had an extra NBC jacket because there was a soldier who didn't have one. As Kimbrough and I looked around we noticed that to the right of us was a soldier who was just sitting in her seat without a jacket. I started to realize that she could be our first casualty as the plane circled around the area. Our training always taught us how to handle battle, but you can't teach your emotions to handle war and they are often more intense than the battle itself. Luckily an ALL-CLEAR directive came over the speakers to say that it was safe to land, but I knew that it was now a matter of life or death.

As we landed in Kuwait, the sandstorms and heat were the first things that struck me as completely different from the terrain of the Mojave Desert, where our units trained before being sent to the Middle East. Kuwait City was well developed, just like cities in the US, but our bases were underdeveloped since they had not been maintained. But we adjusted to that.

As we traveled from Kuwait to Iraq, I started to think about the circle of history from the Greek conquest of the region to the American invasion that I was now part of. The number of destroyed tactical vehicles in Kuwait and Iraq was enormous on Highway 9 as we were escorted into Iraq. The threat level was high, and we were issued two MREs (Meal Ready to Eat) and one liter of water to last us for our 300-mile convoy, which would take us approximately 18 hours, depending on how long it took the convoys before us to secure the route and site.

As we convoyed on the Iraqi highway into Baghdad, we were on the lookout for enemy contact, which we luckily only rarely encountered. But from the corpses along the highway, we knew that numerous engagements had taken place prior to our arrival. This was not something that our training had prepared us for. Along with the smell of burning vehicles, bodies, and animals there was just this aura of death in the air, which gave me a different perspective on life. I learned to appreciate life and see it in a different way. I realized that I no longer cherished normal life in the way that people did back home. With the possibility of death everywhere, every moment mattered to all of us. I realized that "time" was more special to me than money or material things. I wanted to be in a position to be able to do what I want to do with my own time, because our time is usually the one thing that we can control. We live and we die, and we control very little beyond that. Once you see death all around you in warfare, you will see life in a different respect.

The sandstorms made it even more difficult to see our threats. The sky turned red and was full of sand in the heat. We knew that the rifles the Iraqi Army used were far more durable than ours, so we cleaned our rifles in shifts or during every break we had.

Arriving in Baghdad gave us some sense of relief, but we were still on guard because the buildings and homes in the city had numerous windows from which snipers could target us. To live in daily fear of dying heightens your vigilance and awareness. I respect the people back home for pursuing their dreams but it's nothing like meeting another combat veteran who understands your emotions and the way you look at life. I lived in danger in the streets but trust me when I say that it does not compare to combat.

I deployed in March 2003 but was able to leave the combat area to report to my next unit in Germany in October 2003. As that unit was still in Iraq, I took leave to go back to Savannah to see my family. I was welcomed by my family, but they did not throw a party for me or show a lot of excitement for my visit. It was as if I was just on vacation and came back home. My family had no idea what I had to endure in the Middle East, nor did they seem to care.

As I reported to Wiesbaden, Germany the tempo of deployments was increased and my wife was assigned to deploy within the next few weeks for six months, which would leave me in Germany alone for two months until my unit returned. What I noticed immediately in Germany was how much the local nationals loved Black men. My expectation was that many Germans would have Neo-Nazi ideas and would reject us. However, this was far from the truth. In fact, it was common for Black soldiers to retire in Germany. This is when I realized that what I was taught about a place in school and by news outlets was totally different from what that place is like when you actually go there. Germans' perceptions of Black people were based on what they saw or heard in the movies and in music, but once they realized that we are not the media image of ourselves, they embraced us as human beings. Germany was the first place where I saw all different types of Africans and was stunned by their appearance. I only envisioned them in certain ways. This further made me realize how my country limited the truth about other people.

Within the year I deployed again to Iraq, but this time I was sent to Balad, which is in the Sunni triangle and was called the Triangle of Death after the fall of the Ba'athist government. It was the site of major combat activities and sectarian violence from 2003 to 2007. We encountered so many daily mortar attacks on the base that they became normal to us. After a 12-month deployment, I was back with my wife and we had our daughter, whom we named Fa'amalolealofa, which means Thank God for the Love in Samoan. She gave me and received the love that I was missing from and for my mother.

My next duty station was back home in Fort Stewart, Georgia with the 3rd Infantry Division. I loved this division not only because it was in my home state, but because it was where my manhood and understanding of what I was experiencing grew. It was there that I realized that what I learned through school and in American media was all designed to keep me in the system's mental bubble. I didn't see racism in the other countries, but I did see cultural clashes between nationals and foreigners, battles between organized crime groups, and conflicts over perceptions. None of these was as intense as the racism that I felt in the States.

A combat arms unit is very masculine and is all about being intimidating. My unit was all male and predominantly white. There were a few of us Blacks, but we knew we were outnumbered. We heard racial slurs, but we had to either tolerate them or challenge the whites who said them, at the risk of being labeled angry Black men. I knew how to dance in the middle because of my cultural awareness, but I was still not one of them.

There was one incident that really stuck with me. A group of us (two Blacks and five whites) were sitting around a fire pit in Fort Irwin with some officers, including my platoon sergeant, who was from Puerto Rico. My platoon sergeant said to our first sergeant, who was from South Carolina, that he wanted to move to Jesup, Georgia, which was around an hour away from the base. He said, "Hey, I'm going to buy a house in Jesup in your neighborhood, so I can go hunting and fishing with y'all!" As he said this there was an awkward silence for a quick moment and my first sergeant's friend, who was also a first sergeant, said "Bud! Did you tell him where we live? I don't think you want to do that!"

I immediately looked at my platoon sergeant and told him, "Maybe you want to go somewhere else. You know you're not part of that environment, right?" He replied to me, "Shit! I will fly three flags: my American, Puerto Rican, and rebel flag in my front yard!" We all laughed and then the first sergeant's friend replied, "No, I don't think that's a good idea." I understood that there are areas where you see the sign that states "join the Brotherhood" on a Confederate flag and, if you're from Georgia, you understand what area you are in. I'm not saying that those areas are not safe, but I am saying that certain types of idealism don't fly there.

The 3rd Infantry Division was known for spearheading the war in Iraq and for taking part in the major battles there. This was my first time being assigned to a combat unit so now I was on the front lines. This experience taught me the true meaning of brother in arms. Race, creed, religion, or gender did not matter to us. What mattered was if we could trust each other with our lives. As I prepared for my third combat tour into Iraq, part of our training included understanding the culture and history of the region. As I started to do more research on my own and learned that Iraq produced one of the earliest civilizations in the world, dating back to 6,000 BC, I reflected on my own journeys in life. This gave me more insight into humanity and the spiritual journey of life itself. We deployed in Forward Operating Base Falcon, which was eight miles south of Baghdad. We had to deal with numerous mortar attacks there as well but this time we took some casualties. This was the first time that I witnessed one of our own lose their life and it was truly a sad experience.

As part of the counterinsurgency program implemented by US Forces in Iraq, our units were made to live side-by-side with Iraqis in their neighborhoods. Our neighborhood was the province of Hawr Rajab, which is right outside of Baghdad. My interaction with the Iraqis was like being among people back home but just in a different environment. I learned not to see them as the enemy but as human beings whose lives have been interrupted by governments whose policies have forced them to change their society, economy, and ideals. Most of the American soldiers who were deployed in Iraq were so angry about 9/11 and about fellow soldiers who lost their lives there that they were blind to the Iraqis' true humanity.

We spent over 14 months in Iraq before returning home and I experienced a new appreciation for life as a result. I started by apologizing to every family member for my own wrongdoings. I was not necessarily asking for their forgiveness but hoping to forgive myself and free myself of the guilt I carried. Most of my family didn't even remember some of things I was apologizing for, but I wanted to be free of the burden.

Before I retired, I spent five years in South Korea, where I learned about the Japanese colonization of Korea and its wartime policy of forcing Korean women into sex slavery ("comfort women"). I took numerous historical tours of South Korea and saw the impact that Japanese colonialism had on Korea. It reminded me of what I knew already about the Black experience in America.

While stationed in Korea I went back to Okinawa for the first time since my last visit when I was 16 years old. I was 40 years old at the time. I was very nervous about whether my family would accept me after all these years, but I was welcomed. My mother had aged drastically since I had last seen her; she even looked older than my father, who was ten years her senior. I healed completely by going back to my birth country and now I felt whole. I returned to Okinawa one more time before leaving Korea and I accepted the fact that this visit could be my last.

As my reconnection with my family in Okinawa grew, I started to speak to them often through an app called LINE every morning. One day I was on the phone with my family while I was entering my office where I worked with 3 other Americans and 11 Korean nationals. As I was talking on the phone, I realized that all the Koreans got up from their cubicles and gathered in a huddle while glancing in my direction. As the second in charge, I thought nothing of it because I knew that they were competent employees who rarely made mistakes. But Mr Kim, whose cubicle was next to mine, asked me if I spoke Japanese. I replied that my mother is Okinawan. With that, he asked if I could speak Japanese outside the office because hearing Japanese offended him and our other Korean co-workers. At that moment I realized the history behind all the racial jokes about Koreans that I used to hear in my family's household, which I always used to believe was just competitive talk between nations. It was after that experience that I decided to learn the truth about the horrific actions that Japan had taken against the Koreans. Learning that history, and continuing to build positive relationships with them and other Korean people, was my way of apologizing to my Korean co-workers for what some Japanese people had done to their people and country.

9

In Silicon Valley*

In Silicon Valley, I am 23 and starting a graduate program in engineering at Stanford. I live in a pool house in Atherton, where I have just finished writing a bad novel and being a nanny—temporarily playing a stay-at-home mom.

In Silicon Valley, it is 1995. I have just discovered a new drug called Prozac, and I am sure my real life is about to begin. I want to be a professor. I don't know any entrepreneurs.

In Silicon Valley, it is pre-almost everything. Larry Page and Sergey Brin are developing PageRank, which will enable Google two years later. eBay has just been launched as an unknown online service called Auction Web. We buy our books at the bookstore, our toilet paper and toothpaste at CVS. Mark Zuckerberg is 11 years old.

In Silicon Valley, I meet Noah at the department mixer on the first day. After two hours, while the guys next to us debate the viability of a new company called Amazon, Noah says, "You know we're going to fuck." I'm there to work hard and ensure myself a career, to prove I am brave and strong, not to fuck. But within a week we fall into the kind of barrel wave love that, in addition to the Prozac, temporarily annihilates all my adolescent and

---

* Some names have been changed

young adult questions of authenticity—Am I sick or am I sane? Am I good or am I bad?—and then, we do.

In Silicon Valley, the dot-com bubble inflates with us inside it, and I inhale ambition like the sweet-tasting nitrous oxide I learned to crave after knocking out my two front teeth on a diving board when I was ten. It is really good shit, and I pivot my plan to profess and take a job at Cisco. I travel around the world and teach men about the best way to run their Internet backbone. In Tokyo, Sao Paolo, Beijing, and Herziliya, men buy me lunch and ask my opinion, and I let them. I like the way this makes me feel smart. In Vegas, I work the product booths at COMDEX and CES and men mistake me for a "booth babe" while I talk about router speed. They say, "You sure don't look like an engineer", and I'm not offended. Yet. Instead, I like the way this makes me feel special.

In Silicon Valley, it is the year 2000. I marry Noah in a Jewish-like ceremony by a pool in Menlo Park. We sell some stock to pay for the wedding. The rabbi I find on the Internet marries us with generic vows that I Google, and all four of our divorced parents walk us down the aisle. After the wedding, I sell my consignment-store-bought dress on eBay for three times what I paid for it. On our honeymoon in Italy, I use the money I make to buy sensible shoes I will wear to work for decades. This will remain the proudest financial exchange of my life for a long while, because it is public, and because I believe it reflects the way I want to be seen: rational and non-materialistic—unconcerned enough with my appearance to buy a second-hand wedding dress for $200 (though, as I am quick to point out, it was brand new with the $2,000 price tag still on it)—and less than extravagantly privileged. I tell the story often.

In Silicon Valley, I give birth to Wilson, take six months of maternity leave, and then stop traveling. I edit data sheets in my felt-walled cubicle while Wilson sits in the daycare at my office building, down the hall. I watch an image of him in the corner of my computer screen and feel sad, although it's not because I think he's not being well cared for. It's because I realize I no longer give a fuck about the Cisco 12000 Gigabit Switch Router, but I still want my career. I am terrified of failing as Wilson's mother. I am sure his three months of constant colic screaming must have been partially my fault. I was nervous and weepy in those months at home, while Noah was stalwart and calm. Noah and Wilson are good, but what if I'm bad? My work shines like armor, protecting me and legitimizing my worth. We have apartment rent to pay, too.

In Silicon Valley, it is 2004. I give birth to Ben and my boss lets me work from home three days a week. I do gymnastics class with Wilson and read him books at library time and teach him how to head a soccer ball. Ben smiles along with us around town in his Baby Bjorn: it is pre-Bugaboo stroller. My confidence grows, and also, my joy. Wilson memorizes professional soccer players' names from around the world and yells "Zambrotta! Did you see that?" as he scores in the small goal in our new foam-covered playroom/garage. Ben learns to climb the step ladder and dunk basketballs in the plastic hoop. "Boom!" Ben says. "Basket. See that?" I see and cheer them on.

I abuse the work deal and use a lot of that time to play with my sons and train for Olympic-distance triathlons. I am ashamed of the cheesy clip art I shove into slides to mask lack of content or zeal. I train harder and win a few races. These victories soothe the shame.

Then the HR guy calls me in. "We'll need you to work harder", the soft-talking 20-something in Dockers and a faded polo shirt tells me. "In the office, every day." I am relieved by the impossible ultimatum. "I quit", I say. It is the easiest decision I've ever made. I am so privileged to have the savings and stock from Cisco to make it. HR tries not to flinch, but I see it and it is pleasing. This can't be my story, but neither, I tell myself, can staying home.

In Silicon Valley, I'm 33 and I can see what it takes to be special. I decide to learn how to be an entrepreneur.

I share a garage in Palo Alto with two other startups. *The San Francisco Chronicle* comes to the garage to photograph me for a story. The story says I'm a "local powermom" because I'm an entrepreneur, mother, and feminist who organizes events that demand equal pay and fair time off for mothers. I work around the clock with my kids in tow and don't earn much money. I only organize the one event the article talks about.

In Silicon Valley, my business partner, Abby, gives me 20 per cent of the company when I join, and an iPhone for Christmas so that I never have to miss anything ever again. I take up the habit of refreshing my email every three minutes. I wake at four in the morning and roll over to look at it. The unread messages are like pills that pack a quick hit—popping bright, white, and oblong.

The New York Times does a story on my partners and me. We are three moms making a BPA-free baby bottle shaped like a breast. Actually, we are remaking it. Abby is the daughter of the original founder. Her dad shot himself but left a note asking Abby to quit her job as counsel at Yahoo! and reinvent his boutique baby bottle business. She says the company had nothing to do with his death, that he was sick already, and that she, too, is sick of the round-the-clock legal work at Yahoo! So that's what she's doing: reinventing the bottle. I help her.

In Silicon Valley, I see my picture in the paper and my product in the display windows. My boys ooh and squeal.

We win a design award for the bottle, which prompts the *Times* story. The other winner of the award that year is the iPhone. Whole Foods sells the bottle, which makes me feel like maybe this time, I'm for real. I take Wilson and Ben to the Palo Alto store to see it when it goes up on display. We walk along the unfamiliar aisles that smell grainy and sweet, like wet earth and granola, until we find the bright blue and orange packaging. I take pictures of Ben and Wilson standing in front of the rungs and rungs of product with the logo I made and words that I wrote. The feeling of pride—of seeing my precious boys smile in the same frame with my plastic bottles is warm and dizzying, like the flush of an epidural or three glasses of wine.

Target sells the bottle, too. But the week after they begin offering it, Abby accuses me of sleeping with a potential investor I only swim with and fires our third partner. The next month, I quit. Abby sells the company for the price of its patents. None of us make a dime.

In Silicon Valley, I parlay my baby bottle failure into another startup I didn't conceive of. I am flown to New York by another set of venture capitalists, who have already funded an entrepreneur in Manhattan named Philippa. For five years, I co-found companies with Philippa, and am funded by Dan and Samir. Our first two shut-downs are seen as almost necessary entrepreneurial chops, temporary injuries, even valuable expertise. Most startups shut down, and, in Silicon Valley, venture capitalists actually like to see that their founders can change course quickly and start up again, despite public humiliation and internal pummeling.

This is called pivoting. I pivot well.

Our third company soars. Philippa and I hire an evangelical youth group leader who lives in Texas and drives a pink Hummer to run sales. She says things like, "I'm praying a lot this week", instead of, "Here's what the numbers say", as we lead up to earnings reviews. We bring Mandy to a pitch on Sand Hill Road. She says, "I know God put me on the earth to build this sales force." I clench my teeth.

"Now that's good backing", the venture capitalist says with a wink.

Despite Mandy, or perhaps because of her, we raise $6 million. I hire 50 employees and we sit in a new office with two break rooms and a receptionist desk. We fill only one break room with peanut butter pretzels, popcorn, and Snapple, and we never have a receptionist. Philippa doesn't move here. She stays in Manhattan with her kids. I make it home to mine when their school day ends, and work again when they sleep.

In Silicon Valley, local business owners know my company. For a time, my employees love me. I love them back. I pay them well. I buy birthday cakes and cards and give rewards for forthrightness. I am a good mother to them, and to my boys. I am aware that I can afford to be, but just barely.

My content manager, who works from home because she's a mom with four young kids and a husband who doesn't make a tech salary, posts on Facebook: "I just saw my baby's first steps thanks to my flexible job. Thank you, Philippa and Sarah." I'm proud of this.

In Silicon Valley, my community knows me. My friends and family buy my company's deals and help me promote them. I feel like a local hero. There is joy and eroticism in the work, and also in the coming-back-home. I feel connected by a live wire threaded straight through the heart. I feel like a teenager, out late after dark with a boy, listening to "Young Turks" by Rod Stewart.

In Silicon Valley, I wake daily at 4 a.m., roll away from my sleeping husband, kiss my sons' foreheads, and tiptoe down the stairs to rendezvous with my inbox, where 50 or 60 new emails await me. I answer them immediately. In the glow of the moon and the glare of the iMac screen I fire off decisions and congratulate myself for my enterprise and deed.

At 5:30, I drive to the public community center in my swim parka with my work outfit, swim bag, laptop case, and handbag piled beside me. In the pool, I swim several miles, digging deep beneath the surface to feel my body burn and then to let my limbs go loose in the water, to undulate and play. Thoughts of new website icons and marketing messages ping against my pink goggles in uncanny video images as I slice through the bioluminescent-lit pool in the dark. Slights from my investors, like "I'll do this presentation for you, you don't need to talk", slingshot through my biceps like rubber bands and I slap my wrists against the water, then carve them deep in hourglass figures, down. *I can speak*, they pull. *I just have something different to say.*

When the moon starts to fade, I hoist myself out of the vat of blue and head for the locker room consumed with the business decisions at hand. In the communal shower I scald my lactic muscles and chat about swim sets and life setbacks with my Masters fellow teammates, each of us halfheartedly lamenting our age. The truth: I feel high. Then I dress. I am known for getting out the door before anyone else is out of a towel. *You're so fast, Sarah!* they say. *Slow down.* I just wave and get off.

By 7:00, I've procured my favorite coffee and gooey blueberry molasses muffin (which I eat only the top of) from Café Borrone, and am speeding toward the office in San Mateo with a drenched shirt collar. I am efficient: productive, if not well coiffed. I refuse to waste the last few moments before dawn blow-drying my hair. It is the darkness and emptiness of the streets I love most about mornings just after my swim, as if in that town of early risers, supermoms, and overnight successes, I alone have beat the sun.

At the office, I fire off more emails, review the latest launch schedules, give talks via Skype to the sales force, prep for upcoming partnership pitches, have one-on-one reviews with direct reports, and eat the bottom of my blueberry muffin, which I have saved for just this purpose, with a cup of stale coffee for lunch. Eating feels almost irrelevant. I do not have to fill food journals, or fret over whether taking one more bite of Grape Nuts makes me weak. Entrepreneurship is like a round-the-clock, all-I-can-eat validation buffet.

In Silicon Valley, our third company begins to pivot toward decline. I have to lay off my content manager who works from home, and our HR manager, who threatens to sue us when we lay her off in the third round. We hire a temp to help with the rest of the layoffs.

Then Dan and Samir fire Philippa, replace her with a wildly successful herbal supplement salesman named "Chaz". A few months later they fire me and alert us both there will be no further pay or severance, and force us to sign away our equity. We don't make a dime.

This is called failing.

Still, in Silicon Valley, entrepreneurs are judged not by whether we fail, because we all do, but by how we respond to failure. Business failure is the kind I am not only resilient to but secretly crave: it holds no candle to much deeper fears. So, I expect to fail well. But I don't. Not really. This failure is what unleashes the shame. Again.

What happened? People ask when they see me at school pickup. What now? I tell my story over and over, but I don't really tell it. I explain in plain English that I had a disagreement with the investors, or with the business model. I say I was done wasting my time on lame daily deals—who were we to think we could compete with Groupon? What good were we doing the world? I'd always wanted to write, anyway. Other times I describe how proud I am of what we built together for our employees—a distributed sales force that gave hundreds of women part-time flexible work and helped local businesses—but claim I am passing the torch, taking a break, coming home to be with my boys more, take them surfing, to soccer practice, to the library, and make better food. To play, to nourish, to love, and to learn.

In the first few weeks, I get asked by other entrepreneurs to start other companies, and I'm tempted. Soon, I run into a friend named Lisa. She's self-funding a new venture and she asks me to be her partner. For two days, I consider it. One night, I have two dreams. I dream that I'm on the front page of *Time* magazine with Lisa, and then I dream that I call up my investors and say, "Hey, listen up. I made it after all." On the second day, I swim for two hours instead of one hour because I can't stop. In the shower, I feel alive again, like before, but then the endorphins wear off and I feel like my normal self again, which is low and confused. But I do realize I don't give a fuck about Lisa's business, or co-founding any more tech businesses at all, ever.

This discovery terrifies me. If my response to failure is to drop out of the tech world I no longer want to inhabit, will that teach my Silicon Valley boys that I'm a quitter, that I am weak? If I pivot my striving toward something less measurable, perhaps more tender and deeper than product launches and fundraising, will my sutures rip open and expose some condemnable yearning I don't want to see? Or expose something condemnable in the achievement-oriented privileged striving I have submerged myself, and my family, in? I do not yet see the broader signs that, in a lot of ways, we are all coming undone.

In Silicon Valley, I do not yet know enough to ask the right questions or pause to wonder what the risks and outcome of this operation might be. I do not yet know enough to ask what I might gain. Instead, I wonder: if the treatment is examining the cult of the extreme, then after the anesthesia wears off, will I regret living here and staying to raise my sons? Will I be black-balled or shamed into silence by those who don't agree with what I expose? Or, as I later learn to ask, will I stay and continue to speak, fear and shame be damned, both for my boys and for everything that is larger than my own family? What will I lose by re-opening my own heart?

From the car I call Lisa and say no to her partnership offer. There's really only one thing I can do. I am privileged to be able to do it. I go home to figure out who I've become.

10

Bootstraps (work hard and be nice)

Ten-year-old Wilson tilted away from me on the two back legs of his chair and balanced there with the ease of a water buoy. He was studying, as was his routine before he ate his after-school snack, and I'd begun to notice the haphazard collage of our photos I posted to the bulletin board on the adjacent wall. I leaned toward him from across our kitchen-cum-dining room table.

After a moment he plunked down on all four legs and stripped off his favorite white Stanford tee, then seemed to focus on the image I never switched out: a year-old picture taken during a launch celebration at my office. In it my husband, Noah, my younger son, Ben, and Wilson are shoveling huge chunks of what looks like bright pink wedding cake into our open smiling mouths; in the background, my co-founder, my employees, my family, and friends—nearly everyone I love in my Silicon Valley circle—are grinning at us, blurrily displaying teeth tinged pink with sugar and wine.

"That was a good cake", Wilson reminisced.

"It's good I'm home now", I said, mostly to myself, though I nodded at the premade burrito I'd managed to heat for him. He looked at me with his deep-blue, diving pool eyes.

"I kind of wish you had a job still", he said.

"Why…" my stomach sank and my voice caught, "…do you say that?"

Wilson looked down, poked the burrito, and then his neck lengthened somehow. We had surprised one another, but he was an honest boy. He gazed up at me. "Because then our whole family would be successful."

"What", I said, and I wanted to add, the hell did you just say? But I dutifully refrained.

Wilson was assessing my reaction, watching my shoulders, which had begun to droop. "Mom," he said. "It's not bad." His regret was elephantine; I knew I should rescue him. He was ten, and a patch on his smooth white neck was beginning to flush cardinal. His collarbone seemed to curl around his sternum and cave his chest inward, as if in an attempt to protect his whole heart, and he glanced across the floor at his shirt, as if he just wanted to put it back on. But I was angry. Not at him, but at everyone.

"I mean, your company was cool", Wilson said. "I liked it. And Dad's is cool too."

"I know", I agreed. "But I like this, too." And I did like being with him. But I hadn't known it would feel so much like shame.

In the past 20 years, I'd studied engineering, traveled the world training men on Internet routing technology, and co-founded three companies. In the past 30 days, I'd been ousted from my own company, and learned that going from running an office full of people eager for one's opinion to eating a peanut butter and jelly sandwich alone in the kitchen feels oppressive and dire.

This was not real oppression, and to use the word "dire" is too bleak. I had ample choice in the matter; I could afford to stay home. I also could have gone right back to my striving. And yet, I vaguely knew getting another tech job would just make things worse. I wasn't yet sure why.

Wilson nodded. "Sorry", he said. "Why'd I say that?" He duck-dived beneath the wave of tension I hated myself for having formed and brought his face down to the burrito instead of lifting it up to his mouth. He took a bite, and I stifled a sob.

The sign on the wall behind Wilson's head said, "Work Hard and Be Nice" in big white letters on dark gray wood. This passed for art in our house, and for religion. I had chosen it on a lunch break years ago and hung it in my home's most visible spot like a cross.

I knew that we need to hold these values in at least equal measure; that success in life is about personal striving, but it is also more importantly about being kind. As an entrepreneur I was known mostly for my hard work: a limited virtue. Once home, I worried that I would be known only for being nice, although I so often felt pissed off at myself and unlikable.

"It's okay, buddy", I said, thinking: I'm sorry, Wilson. I could see that he knew I was lying, and he didn't like it. I wanted to tell him it was not a lie but a half-truth. What he had said was okay. But increasingly, I was not. Because although I so badly wanted to feel good enough, my gut said he was right. I was newly 40, and a failed entrepreneur. Without a title or a paying job, I felt as if, aside from my life with my family, I did nothing. I produced nothing. I only consumed. This made me feel both worthless and extravagantly self-centered. I was not enough for Silicon Valley, and motherhood was not enough for me.

Here is what I imagined Wilson innocently asked of me: Why don't you have a job like Dad? I thought you were good at it. I thought you loved running a company. So, tell me, Mom, if you're not working and productive now, then what was it all for? What are you now?

"Come on," I said, "eat." Wilson had soccer practice in an hour, and I needed him to feel strong.

I wondered how long that sign would haunt me. There was no fucking chance I was taking it down.

It's possible that when Wilson said he wished our whole family were successful, he meant he wished our whole family were accomplished. But later, I began to wonder if it was something more generous, and also more alarming. I began to think he could see that I wasn't feeling good, and he didn't like it. But instead of saying he wished our whole family were happy, he said "successful". Maybe he chose "successful" because achievement was what he identified with most as making me happy. Maybe the kind of extreme striving for success we worship in Silicon Valley today was already the main thing he'd identified that would make him happy and define him as good enough.

That, I think, is what scared me.

The American heritage is work hard and maintain a high moral code and you, too, can achieve "the good life" American Dream. But while we often equate this "dream" with the positive-sounding platitude "Work Hard and Be Nice", and a moderate life, I think it's worth examining where this ethic actually came from, and the fact that it isn't always associated with doing particularly good work, or with being kind.

Manifest Destiny legitimized the idea that God had ordained the white protestant male as worthy and good with a boundless right to pillage and conquer. This limitlessness inspired a long tradition of dichotomous either–or thinking. If you happen to be able to amass increasing power or profit, you're good. If you're not, then you're told you're bad. But truly being kind—to ourselves, to our children, to others—requires being open to the fluidity between good and bad; it requires real compassion, and more than a single definition of what success or "good" means. The high moral code of Manifest Destiny was and is, instead, a bit less generous, a bit more circular: keep the momentum of white protestant imperialism going.

Silicon Valley likes to present itself as a meritocracy, as if equal opportunity abounds and the only excuse for getting nothing out of the system, for not eventually achieving success, is lack of ambition and drive: a failure to work hard enough or be good enough. We know this is bullshit. We know that in the same twisted, complex way that worth is tied to wealth in America, so are race, environmental justice, and education. We know that access to clean air and water and to education is largely dictated by zip codes, not ambition or drive, or a willingness to work. We know that less privileged kids are dying for less glamorized and privileged reasons than striving, by others' hands as well as their own. We know, or we should know, that our educational system was set up this way on purpose, the same way redlining and housing restrictions segregated our neighborhoods on purpose. So why do we perpetuate the myth of meritocracy by not explicitly speaking out and working against it? One answer to that question is difficult to admit but easy to conjure: for years, I pardoned the meritocracy myth because my sons and I benefitted from it. Or I thought we did.

"This is the mythography of America, progressive," Junot Diaz says, "where you have this idea that everything moves upward, and people are always on this journey to improvement." At every turn we are asked and meant to know: either we're on the journey toward success and perfection and we're good, or we're not, and we're bad. "The transcendence myth", Diaz says, "will just do you in, in the long run."

I would witness this undoing. My husband curled in the fetal position on the couch, instead of going to his job at Amazon, depressed and burnt out. My dear friend in the hospital after being convinced she was worthless both at home and at work. My chauffeuring of a friend to ECT treatments and ketamine drips to lift catatonic despair, and news of 5150 holds and overcrowded mental health clinics around the Bay. Many children I love on meds, sent away for treatment, or caught with underbed hidden blades. Wilson's teammate lost to suicide a few short months before Covid hit, during his senior year in high school. And me. I was undone.

I know that the dangers of excess are real and present for my family and me. But it is rarely only ourselves we do in when we live in the extreme. This is especially true on the privileged side. With privilege comes the power to set expectations and culture, and to effect change. Whom else do we mother, or care for by extension, when we mother our daughters and our sons? For whom else are we setting expectations? I don't mean to say that other children, or mothers, are dependent on privileged white strivers to succeed. But how did we get here, and how can our mothering be at once more revolutionary and less extreme?

In the winter of 2017, when swastikas were showing up on the Santa Clara University campus (and seemingly everywhere else), and fake news was the "next big thing", our local paper ran a story about the district's decision to change the names of the two "high performing" public middle schools in West Palo Alto: Terman Middle School and Jordan Middle School, both of which feed into Palo Alto High. Back in 2016, a student had done a book report on his school's namesake, David Starr Jordan, and the nearby school's namesake, Lewis Terman. *Lewis Terman?* I'd thought. The names were being changed, it seemed, because both men had been instrumental in the American eugenics movement. Eugenics?

I'd never thought much about Jordan Middle School and who it was named after, but I'd always assumed Terman Middle School was named after Frederick Terman, like the Terman engineering building at Stanford where I fell in love with Noah and reckoned with supply chain economics and multivariable calculus and could practically spit at from the Stanford Hospital maternity ward.

Frederick Terman is widely credited, along with William Shockley, as "the father of Silicon Valley". He was Stanford's School of Engineering dean for a time, and the author of the seminal textbook *Radio Engineering* in 1932. Frederick Terman was, and still is, regarded as the original cream of the Silicon Valley crop: an elite intellectual and an entrepreneurial pioneer.

Lewis Terman, whom I had to look up, was Frederick Terman's father: a Stanford psychologist who pioneered intelligence testing. In the early 1900s, he co-authored the Stanford–Binet scales, which we still use nationwide today (in its much revised edition) to diagnose developmental or intellectual "deficiencies", and genetic intellectual "superiorities", in young children. He is known as the father of modern IQ testing. And his friend and colleague David Starr Jordan, Stanford's first president, pioneered the notion of "race and blood" in his 1902 seminal text on using eugenics to engineer a Master (white) Race: *The Blood of the Nation: A Study in the Decay of Races by the Survival of the Unfit*. He claimed that things like talent and poverty and intelligence could be inherited by blood and advocated for breeding them in and out of the human race as a practice. Both Terman and Jordan were active members of the American Eugenics Society.

"That's an awesome responsibility," a local hospital commercial voiceover from this time croons, "not just for a place, but for the people that live there. To be the custodians of such remarkable promise, bringing them into the world, helping them grow, and fulfill all the potential that their parents imagine. Proudly caring for Northern California, birthplace of pioneers."

This got me thinking about who we call pioneers, and what responsibility we have to interrogate those America has praised.

Eli Whitney "pioneered" the cotton gin on Mulberry Grove Plantation, in what is now Port Wentworth, Georgia, in 1793.

Mulberry Grove was among the first estates to have its marsh acreage cultivated for rice production, and to prosper. When the rice market fluctuated, cotton was experimented with. The cotton gin was invented during this time. It revolutionized the way cotton was harvested, shaped the economy of the Antebellum South, and reinvigorated slavery.

Less than a mile away, my five times great-grandfather, George Paul Keller, married Catharine Strobhar (1763–1834), who owned the 500-acre Salem Plantation, in Port Wentworth. Catharine had inherited it from her father, a wealthy planter who had moved there from Purisburg, South Carolina and owned a great deal of land in Georgia and South Carolina, and over 35 enslaved humans, immense wealth by the standards of colonial Georgia. Salem was primarily a rice plantation; 17 people were enslaved on it in 1796. In the early 1790s, George went off with the state militia to "fight the Indians".

I have my ancestors' wills and birth certificates and slave schedules and I have additional context thanks to my mother's late best friend and second cousin, Andy Lewis, who took oral histories of our ancestors who were still alive in 1966 and then wrote a 30-page paper full of truth telling.

George and Catherine had four children, one of whom was my four times great-grandfather, John Adam Keller. From Andy's paper: *John Adam Keller was a hot-tempered fellow who got violent when angry. He died in 1830, and was buried on his plantation. The records of his estate show that he was the first in the family to adopt the cruel practice, continued by his sons, of renting out the labor of slaves he was not using at the time. At the time of his death, he owned twenty-two slaves, who had multiplied into thirty by the time the estate was divided; he also had seven hundred acres of land in Chatham County and considerable holdings elsewhere.*

Around 1814, John Keller married Levisa (Levicy) Peeples (1798–1863). One of their three sons was George Adam Keller, my great-great-great-grandfather.

My mother was proud of telling me that I'd scored highly on the pre-kindergarten IQ test and thought it fantastic that my public school had the GATE "Gifted and Talented" program that gave me and the other "high IQ" kids extra classes and activities, and I'm sure I agreed with her. Maybe it was fantastic, mostly. I certainly felt smart, and special, and I never felt my gender disadvantaged me. My mother recently told me, when I asked about it, that so many kids at my school scored in the "gifted" range that the entire school received extra funding. For a second, that made me feel great: in that white bubble, we were all treated special! The obvious problem, of course, was that the "non-gifted" schools and students in other areas were not.

My affluent white friends and I benefitted while the less afflu-ent and mostly non-white children did not, often resulting in the practice of "tracking" whereby more prepared students took high-level college courses in high school, and less prepared stu-dents took lower-level high school courses that excluded them from college eligibility and/or inspiration. Tracking didn't stop in the 1970s, of course. At my sons' public high school, freshmen come in already tracked into different levels of English, math, and science classes. In 2017 there were only a handful of kids from the East side in the higher-level courses.

The word eugenics was coined in 1883 by the English scientist Francis Galton, a cousin of Charles Darwin. Galton theorized that if gifted and talented people married and reproduced only with one another, the result would be "better" offspring: a sort of "reproduction of the smartest" twist on survival of the fittest, a somewhat subtle form of "positive" eugenics. But his ideas were imported to the United States—a country with a constitution that states "all men are created equal"—right around the turn of the century, and they coincided with two things: Mendel's scientific discovery of the fundamental laws of genetic inheritance and a precarious socio-economic and political climate.

The Radical Reconstruction era ended in the late 19th century with a general feeling of economic resentment among southern whites for "their losses" and soon Jim Crow, a colloquial term for the forms of systemic discrimination via laws and customs that served to discriminate against Blacks, was born. In 1896, *Plessy v. Ferguson* held that the Civil Rights Act of 1875 was unconstitutional and legalized racial segregation, which fueled an already charged atmosphere of extremist racism within our white supremacist systems and culture and a rise in lynching, rioting, and the Ku Klux Klan, whose stated purpose was to intimidate the southern Black population—and any white people who would help them—and to keep that "inferior race" from enjoying basic civil rights. By the start of the First World War in 1914, every Southern state had passed laws that created two separate societies: one Black, the other white.

Simultaneously, American eugenicists suggested that Galton's idea, combined with Mendel's principles of heredity, meant that "undesirable" human traits such as "feeblemindedness", "idiocy", perplexing illnesses like epilepsy, and even "poor morals" or ambition that resulted in things such as promiscuity and poverty could be "bred out", the same way we could genetically determine the color of peas, corn, or cattle. If certain races were "undesirable", could women who would potentially give birth to more babies of those races be sterilized and thus the race "bred out?"

The 1915 World's Fair, which showcased various industrial, educational, artistic, and scientific discoveries from around the world, was held in San Francisco, and one of the most popular exhibits that year was a booth promoting the eugenics movement. It is perhaps too horribly easy in retrospect to understand why. In the midst of a national vulnerability, it was not surprising, although disappointing, that many Americans latched on to concepts of segregation and elitism—*For the betterment of the nation! To Make America Great Again!*—as arguments for peaceful coexistence in the future.

Andy writes: *In 1847, George Adam Keller bought "Coldbrook" plantation, a tract of 1,200 acres, paying for it, it was said, with his wife Martha's dowry. They lived there the rest of their lives. As the Civil War approached, George became active in the Democratic Party, a reflection of his political views. When Georgia seceded from the Union, he joined the state militia with the rank of quartermaster of his regiment, and was later commissioned a captain; he was also a Confederate justice of the peace. He actually served some active duty, but returned home because of an illness.*

After the war, George rose every day, put on his coat and tie, and supervised the plantation in the manner of a gentleman-farmer—largely from the porch. From there he could signal the workers that their lunch hour had come by blowing a horn; there was an overseer to handle the less gentlemanly aspects. George gave the impression of being what one of his granddaughters called an "absolute lord and master," though others in the family believed that the real strength came from his wife, Martha. George buried people who died when there was no preacher, advised his neighbors on politics, and even played doctor and dentist to them. His daughters used to have the scales on which he measured calomel—which he called "blue mash"—and the pliers with which he pulled teeth. In spite of the Civil War, Negroes still lived in the old slave quarters, and there was still a Negro child armed with a fan to keep the flies away when the family sat at table. In the evening, Grandpa would seat himself in the living room, with a Negro boy squatting on either side of his chair, and read and declaim to the family from the daily newspaper.

In Silicon Valley and in America today, we're not yet talking openly about anything as glaringly morally reprehensible as ethnic cleansing. (Are we?) And we know better than to treat human beings as if they are subhuman pets. (Don't we?) But if we can breed humans unencumbered by disability, mental illness, or other disease—if we can eradicate what society deems as imperfection—should we? How will perfection or goodness be defined? Will everyone get this special treatment? Who can afford it? Who held the power on plantations and who holds the power of our nation, still, today?

It took me three years after that first conversation with Wilson, but I took down the sign. I did this even though I understood that there wasn't anything inherently wrong with it. The problem isn't that we want our children to "work hard and be nice". It's in the way that "work" and "nice" and "our children" are defined. I saw that I had a different, much harder kind of work to do if I wanted to stop passing shame down the line. To begin with, I had to keep sitting down to talk with my sons often, and I had to tell the whole truth. I preferred not to do it while staring at false-feeling quotes.

11
400 years to today (Black pride)

Now, here I am in the year of 2019, 400 years after American slavery began, and I am in contact with Sarah Eisner, who is the descendant of George Adam Keller, who was my great-great-great grandfather's owner. It's even hard to say "slave owner".

When I came back home after my five-year tour in South Korea, with plans to retire in 2020, I didn't know where my life would lead. I always knew in my heart that I was here for some higher purpose, and being a soldier, I always wanted to inspire others, but I wanted to inspire small groups at a time, which I believe is the more effective way of inspiring others. Toward this goal, I took the step of returning to Savannah so that I could take on the responsibility of moving my family forward, as my father and his siblings were getting older. I wanted my generation to take the mantle and run with it for our family.

One day I opened my email and I saw an unfamiliar name that hadn't gone to spam. It was an email asking if I was related to Andrew Quarterman, Sr. When I read the email, I was excited, but at the same time I was very nervous. I started to tell my father, my aunts, and my uncle about the message. My uncle was the only one as excited as me. The others were looking at me as though they were thinking, "Aww, whatever. There goes Wild Randy focused on something else!" This confused me. I was wondering why it is that some Black families don't even want to know their pasts. How can we move forward if we don't acknowledge the past?

As my journey to the present day progressed, I began to ask myself many questions and began to see what I think it all meant to me. How did I not become a tragic "statistic"? How did I overcome drug use without any treatment? How did I just stop drinking the way I did without any help? I am lucky, of course, to not have the inherited illness of addiction. A lot of my "luck" comes from the willingness to question the ways things are and to become self-aware; to try to understand who "Randy" is and be honest with myself without apologizing to anyone. It comes from my upbringing in *bushido* ways (the samurai code of honor and morals) that kept me grounded in some way, and which I needed to return to. And from the "wild" way of thinking and doing things. I started to love my people who had made me doubt myself, instead of hating them. I learned that life was bigger than myself and came to believe that the universe is using us as tools to realize its ends.

Now that I am more self-aware, I can't help but look through the eyes of my own people here in America: other Blacks or African Americans. One thing that helped me see more clearly was reading the "Willie Lynch Letter". This letter, written during slavery, was a guidebook for slaveowners with all the successful methods used by them to control slaves for 300 years. The first thing Lynch describes in the letter is how enslavers should pit the young enslaved against the old and vice versa. When I look back at being raised in the Japanese culture, one thing that is expected of everyone is to respect elders, even if the elder is one year older than you. This respect for age creates a sense of honor in the community and in the nation. The second thing Willie Lynch mentions is using physical differences to create divisions within the enslaved population. He advises enslavers to pit the dark complected slaves against light ones; female against male slaves; and long-haired slaves against short-haired ones. In this description I recognized all that I experienced and witnessed in present-day America. Being half-Japanese, I have been often complimented on my lighter skin color and my "good" hair texture, both of which are considered "preferable" to dark skin and kinky hair.

My father always told me that I was born at a good time, when Blacks were starting to take pride in themselves and love themselves enough to fight the oppressors. Maybe this was instilled in me as a child, but I never knew or understood how to use it. My mother left us when I was eight years old. She faced her own confusion, having had a child with an American and feeling the pressure to become a Japanese American. It was not what she wanted, and I sensed this. As a result, I felt unwanted all my life, but I didn't really understand her reluctance to become Americanized until I lived in America as a teen. It was then that I learned how horrific America can be for a young Black person with the odds stacked against you. I always felt I had to work to be accepted in America in ways that I never had to in Japan. In Japan, the main issue is whether you are doing your best to make your family proud. It wasn't all good (if you weren't succeeding you were just called lazy and dumb for not trying), but in America there were too many unspoken rules, like how to act when confronted by the police or by someone in authority, or how not to act in stores because people may assume you are there to steal. There are plenty more examples I could provide but for me it was all too much to take in until I came to the point that I didn't care about anything and doubted who I was all the time.

I lost over nine years of my life just wandering through trouble and confusion. During this time, I held my first son, and something came over me: he didn't deserve to inherit my self-hate and, if he did, it meant that I had failed him. I thought to myself that he may never experience what I have had by traveling the world, by understanding and living in other cultures, and by experiencing a free mind, because he would be raised in America.

What does the reparations land that was given to Zeike Quarterman mean to me?

It means more than life itself!! It means that my family owned something and, even if it is small, it is OURS! I understand that the transatlantic slave trade made money for Europeans and built America, but I want every slave descendant family to be recognized as either workers or contributors to this wealth expansion. The wealth of America was built on the backs of African American families who were sacrificed and who sacrificed everything for it.

Ms Sarah and I spoke every day for a long while. It was like we met before in some previous lifetime. There were so many questions I had for her, but I stuck with our agenda because I didn't know if getting personal would ruin the moment of getting other things right. I had never encountered a white woman in this personal space. It wasn't that I didn't like white people. I'd learned so many life lessons from white people. I was never offended by ignorance because we all need guidance.

When Sarah arrived in Savannah, I was so excited just to feel the vibe she might have. When I saw her, and she had a vase with flowers, I felt very feminine at that time, like wow, I am receiving flowers as a man! But I gave the flowers to my Aunt Priscilla, who was the oldest living Quarterman in our family. When I looked into Sarah's eyes and gave her a hug, I understood we wanted the same thing, which was to uncover the past and truth. My idea was to help the Black community but for her I believe she was trying to move her family into the new way of thinking by acknowledging what was wrong back then.

The next time I encountered Sarah was at an event we both attended. As I looked for her, I felt the excitement of looking for a loved one in a crowd. And when I found her, she was wearing a truck cap, hoodie, jeans, and checkered Vans. Her stepdad and mother, who are equally lovely people, were there too.

The first time Sarah and I shared our story was at a Living Cities meeting, which is a collaboration of 19 of the world's largest foundations and financial institutions working to close the racial income and wealth gaps in American cities. It was Sarah's friend, Nadia Owusu, who introduced us to her colleagues at Living Cities. My uncle, who was 76 years old at the time, and I traveled to New York to share our story and our issue with the property that George A. Keller had given to Zieke Quarterman after the Civil War, which was now threatened by eminent domain. One thing that stuck with me is the question that the board members asked my uncle about his experience during the Jim Crow era. My uncle replied, "I am just a slave. My Daddy told me to never say anything." As a family member I was upset by this answer but, in that moment, I knew that this was the opportunity to show how important education is! My uncle's response was proof of how some rural communities in the South lack adequate schools to overcome feelings of inferiority.

As we left the conference and I looked at my uncle, who was amazed at New York because it was his first time there, I saw him in a different way now, having seen his fear at the conference. I knew at that moment that I had to speak for my family at this forum, not because no one else could but because I had a different view of the situation entirely. I was part of the oppressors as much as I was part of the oppressed. I was taught superiority by being the majority in Japan, not only with respect to Koreans, but also with respect to Japanese Americans, who are looked down upon by the Japanese. This gave me insight into why some Africans viewed us in America in the way they did.

As Sarah and I had more discussions together I became more familiar with her thought process and her intentions to be an example for her sons, which I totally respect. Sarah is on the same journey in life that I am on, and I respect her for that. I don't see her as a white person, but I see her from within and I relate to her goal of being at total peace.

Being connected to Sarah has opened so many doors and she is so vital to this new movement. I don't know if it's fate or our ancestors working through us to do this work, but I can't wait to find out what's in store.

Each mistake teaches you something new about yourself. There is no failure, remember, except in no longer trying. It is the courage to continue that counts.

12
(I hope this is not) white saviorism

In 2019 when I met Randy, the fair market value for the Quarterman land was at least $10,000 an acre, and this value, we would learn, would rise drastically in the following few years given its proximity to port operations. Because the property was owned as heirs' property with a cloudy title, the Georgia Department of Transportation (GDOT) claimed the Quartermans would need to produce a clear title within 12 months in order to receive the lowball fair market price they gave of $2,500. Otherwise, the land would simply be taken and the Quartermans would get nothing. "Good luck", the letter they received with this information read. The Quartermans would be as lucky as possible in this effort, and yet luck has nothing to do with accomplishing an impossible task.

Because Zeike Quarterman had died intestate—without a legal will, as most Black people did in the early 1900s—the Quarterman family owned the ten acres as tenants-in-common, or heirs' property. Heirs' property is land that is passed from generation to generation without a legally designated owner, resulting in ownership divided among all living descendants in a family. Each descendant owns what amounts to shares in a piece of land or property, like a shareholder has in a corporation, but not the actual piece of property. If this sounds confusing, it's because it is. Most attorneys and judges do not understand heirs' property law either. This is part of the problem.

Heirs' property "owners" are limited in what they can do with their land. They aren't eligible to apply for state or federal housing aid (such as funds provided by the Federal Emergency Management Agency), or for nearly any programs administered by the Department of Agriculture. A 2001 report from the US Agricultural Census estimated that about 80 per cent of Black-owned farmland had disappeared in the South since 1969. Approximately half of that land was lost through partition sales. "If the Kennedys, the Bushes, or the Clintons had their property sold or condemned under these circumstances," Thomas W. Mitchell, an expert in heirs' property at the Texas A&M University School of Law, stated, "the law would have been reformed by now."

In September, Randy and I began to consider how his aunt, Priscilla, who'd been paying taxes on the land since her father passed away, might be able to file an affidavit and claim ownership of the land. We each asked family members to tell stories and share information, requested documents from the Chatham County Courthouse and the Georgia Historical Society, did a lot of googling of online databases, and combed through boxes and boxes of collected data. We communicated daily.

In October, I flew to Savannah to meet Randy and members of the Quarterman family at their home in Monteith, along Meinhard Road, to finally meet one another in person, to make the first step toward establishing trust, if that was even possible.

I knew it might not be. I brought my mother and my cousin Bill, both of whom supported this effort, after asking Randy if that was alright.

I was both excited and nervous. I had spent the last month relishing my new, remarkable friendship with Randy. We'd shared photos and stories of our respective families. We'd strategized and researched and been on a conference call together in preparation for our trip to New York City to speak to the heads of national foundations. We needed attorneys to help us to navigate the affidavit process to clear title and to consider litigating the eminent domain issue.

We'd written personal narratives to swap and admire. We'd discussed everything from Southern strictures to national politics and organized religion. Finding one another had been so critically timed with Randy's efforts to save his land that he often said he knew God had brought us together. I called it good research and serendipity and felt compelled to explain that while I respect all religious beliefs, and despite multiple tries, I don't believe in organized religion or God as typically defined. But when Randy replied that he defined God as Love or Vulnerability, it was easy for me to agree that this was the force that had brought us together. In the past few weeks my life had felt more open and generous. It had been filled with more joy, and more love. My relationship with my own mother, whom I was already joined at the heart with, felt even deeper. And I felt my grandmother with us, and even my enslaving ancestors, as if they were on my back, pushing me forward toward healing. More, I felt optimistic about the future of America, and about human connection in general, in places where before I had begun to…not. Even before Randy echoed these sentiments, but I also knew that he was giving me an enormous gift at what might also be a personal cost to him. He didn't need to make reparations. I did. He deserved to retire and rest. Instead, he was doing work that could be retraumatizing for Black Americans and was, at best, often emotionally exhausting.

I tried not to place too much emphasis on what I felt. *This is not about me*, I told myself. But it was unavoidably so of course, at least partially, and it was fraught. Still, I wanted to hear their stories and be as deep as I could in the truth. Relationships are primary in my life, and the only way to have strong ones is to tell our stories.

While I was there, I stayed in our family home on Hilton Head Island, a conflicted story of its own.

When I visited Hilton Head as a child, there was the cinder block beach house in the unplanned area of the island we stayed in, and then there was the other plot of land my grandmother had bought for $5,000 in 1963, maybe a fourth of an acre, just enough for a house and tiny yard, inside a new development called Sea Pines. The lot was overgrown with sweet gum trees, mounds of loblolly pine needles, and Spanish moss. It sat off a cul-de-sac, with road access, and it also had a bumpy cement footpath to the "private" beach. My mother took my brother and me to visit the plot each year, though nothing was on it, to walk on the ground and feel it, to look at the way the ocean looked a few miles down the island from where the current house was, and to touch the sand.

"Someday I hope to build here", she always said, and her eyes would water, and I would hope that it would come true, but it seemed like a distant dream much more than anything that would come to be. "Grandma and Grandpa always wanted this land to be for you someday." Especially after my grandmother died, visiting that land became crucial to my mother. The land was both real and symbolic. It was the raw earth and ocean, and Hilton Head was where her mother was most at ease, and at peace—most like a mother. Maybe that land felt like the closest my mother ever got to getting her mother back from all those sick years. She liked to tell my brother and me how much Grandma wanted us to love it too; how much she wanted to leave this for us, for our children, for our grandchildren; how much she wanted us to know that she had loved us, her only grandchildren, and was so sorry she had never been brave enough to fly and see the land we lived on in California.

The lot sat undeveloped until 1994, when my mother finally sold the cinder block house down the road and used the sale money to build a new one on the lot in Sea Pines. By then, the Sea Pines land was worth more like $500,000 and the taxes were skyrocketing. With her teacher's salary and retirement, my mother kept that house up for over 20 years, renting it out for the 11 or so months a year she couldn't be there to earn the money needed to pay for it, but for the last six she went deeper into debt each year trying to keep up with the rising property taxes. She mortgaged the house again and again while managing renters and trying to let my brother and me go use it one week a year. Then in 2019, my mom told us she couldn't hold on. She needed to put the house on the market. But thanks to Silicon Valley tech luck and striving, I was newly lucky enough to be able to buy our Hilton Head house from my mother so we could keep that land.

The narrative here might be that hard work in the "meritocracy" of Silicon Valley had allowed me to gather enough wealth to sustain the land that my family "owned" and loved—that had always felt most to me like home. And it is true that in co-founding companies, three of which failed (mine) and one of which did well (his), my husband, Noah, and I worked hard, where hard work is defined as mental focus and intellectual rigor, not the brutal physical labor of most low-wage jobs, or the high physical and emotional risks of going to war, like Randy and his father did. It is true that we went without pay for a time and took "risks". We didn't expect to inherit anything from our parents. It's true we'd saved our earlier earnings to make the "risks" possible. It is also true that the white privilege—the privilege of societal safety and deep land-owning roots and good affordable public college education I was able to wait tables to pay for—has always buoyed me up, up, up. The risks we took were quite safe.

The Quarterman family has worked hard too. A majority of the men from Andrew Quarterman Sr's lineage (including Randy and his brother, Aaron Quarterman) have served the city as police officers or the nation in the military. They stuck together and made a priority of close family ties and were able to gain some financial stability. They paid the taxes on that heirs' property every year, and were able to keep it. I don't mean to say that they deserve to keep the land because they worked hard and followed the rules. "Deserve" is often used as a judgement of one's ability to work hard and be nice, and patriotic. The Quartermans must be allowed to keep and control their land because to deny them this would be a cruel act of deprivation, the exact opposite of reparation.

The value of our fourth of an acre and house on Hilton Head today is approximately one million dollars. The narrative might be that the land is and was mine because I paid good money for it. But whose is it really, on a deeper, spiritual level? Is it mine or is it shared? Is it stolen or is it owned? Can it be both? How could I possibly deserve to keep this land more than Randy Quarterman deserves to keep his? How would I feel if someone had denied my family the ability to build on that land? This is the house that my brother and I have now made countless memories in with our mother and with our own sons and daughters. It is where I am most at peace, where I am closest to my sons and to my mother. I cannot imagine my life without that house. And I know it is in no way due to simple "luck" or hard work that I don't have to. Who are the rightful heirs to the property I own?

In 1864, 18 miles from George Adam Keller's Coldbrook Plantation, at Ebenezer Creek, US Union Army Forces engineered a massacre of approximately 10,000 Black formerly enslaved refugees who were following Sherman's March to the Sea. Upon learning of the massacre, in January of 1865, Secretary of War Edwin Stanton asked Sherman to gather a group of 20 men— all Black church leaders, mostly preachers, 16 of whom were formerly enslaved—in Savannah to ask what the government should do for the negroes now that they were free. This led to Sherman's Field Order No. 15, which became known as "40 acres and a mule", though the mule was a myth. The 400,000 acres designated were along the coastline of Georgia and South Carolina, predominantly on Sea Islands, including Hilton Head. A total of

40,000 formerly enslaved people settled on this land before it was promptly taken back and returned to white farmers in April of 1865.

As William A. Darity Jr, professor of public policy and African American studies at Duke University, is quoted as saying: "The origins of the racial wealth gap start with the failure to provide the formerly enslaved with the land grants of 40 acres."

In the closet of the Hilton Head house, the night before I met with Randy's family, my mother and I found a delicate old watercolor map, clearly meant to be wall art, of river plantations neighboring Savannah, including Drakies. Plots of land painted in blue, yellow, green, and pink spanned a wall-length piece of parchment paper. Thousands and thousands of acres of land. White-owned land. Buried in a box, we also found a deed from the early 1900s regarding land that had previously been given from George Adam Keller to one Ellick Sandrich. We had heard tales about an enslaved man the Keller family held in "highest regard" and called "Daddy Ellick" and I assumed Ellick Sandrich was him. The deed for Ellick Sandrich also referenced the Quarterman land—significant because it was legible confirmation of their ownership, whereas the deed that existed for the Quarterman land was illegible in the records even though the promissory note from Keller to Quarterman was legible—and showed that, unlike the Quartermans, who had only begun to lose their land in 2019, Ellick's descendants had lost all their land within one generation. In 1921, after an auction sale that seemed due to unpaid taxes, the land was bought back by a Keller.

At noon, I pulled off the highway at exit 109. I remembered 109 as a quiet green entrance to rural marshland that meandered around to the family cemetery a decade ago, but it was now reputed to be the least desired exit for truck drivers on the eastern seaboard. The volume of port-destined haul traffic was almost too heavy to switch lanes and cross.

"Warehouses", Bill said more than once that day. "Amazon, Wal-Mart, IKEA, Target, you name it. We are becoming warehouses and a port." Blazing red circular logos and haunted smiles hid in the bowels of new warehouse parks, although gas stations, small hotels, and restaurants still lined the main road.

We met Bill and Charlotte at the Sweet Tea Grille, a joint that served tire-sized plates of pulled pork over grits, fried onion strings, and collards renamed as kale in a low-slung building until it went under a few years later during the pandemic. The Bennigans had been there before it had fallen victim to the financial crash of 2008. Sweet Tea was located on a small lane called "Travelers Way" in the shadow of I-95, behind a Shell station and Circle K.

We sat and talked for two hours. The clouds were low and grey, and the humidity and my caffeine-fueled heart rate were raised when we emerged from Sweet Tea. Charlotte explained that she needed to be dropped off at home. She hadn't been to the family cemetery for years, since the day her sister-in-law, Bill's sister, Rebecca, committed suicide. Earlier on that fateful day they'd all gone to the cemetery together and stood looking at cousin Baisley's grave, which Rebecca had been curiously keen to see. Baisley had stepped in front of the train heading into Monteith Station in 1958, on the tracks that ran beside what was now Randy's father's and aunt's land, which they'd built houses on around a man-made lake. The land they lived on, down the street from the heirs' property land, was owned with a clear title. Randy's grandfather had purchased it from a Keller in the 1970s. For over 150 years, the Quarterman family had remained close to their earliest known beginnings: the land deeded to Zeike and Grace.

Baisley's headstone said REST. Baisley's father, my great-great-grandfather, Paul, had suicided with a gunshot to the head in the family barn on Coldbrook in 1904. Rebecca overdosed on pills in the early aughts. Charlotte said the spirits haunted her. Why were those spirits so haunted? What, exactly, was the cause of the Keller curse? How was it being passed down the line and where would it stop?

We dropped Charlotte off at the old farmhouse where Bill farmed banana and bonsai trees in a lush overgrown forested plot framed by a hundreds-of-years-old live oak drenched in moss. We drove, scrunched into Bill's truck, down Meinhard Road and he pointed out properties and locations where the plantations used to be. *This is where the Dotsons lived. This is where the Orrs bought property. That used to be the Hester house and I hear they still own it. All this was part of Coldbrook.* The road was quiet, two lanes. A school bus was behind us. Bill drove slowly, unconcerned.

A mile down the road Bill looked to the right and said: "That's the Quarterman place." He meant the property where Randy's father and aunt lived now. A small praise house sat on a well-tended lawn with a home behind it, and a good-sized, man-made lake behind that, and another home. The property was well-manicured, fronted by the two-lane highway and the rail-road tracks on each side. "That's Baisley's train crossing", Bill said.

We drove to the end of the road where the entrance to Drakies, which George Adam Keller purchased in 1872, used to be. It was still undeveloped, though you could no longer drive in through what used to be the long dirt road. My mother reminisced about being brought to Drakies during times when her mother had needed to go to the hospital to "rest", about the old house she remembered, and the love she'd received, both from her grandparents and from an elderly Black woman named Mrs Mary Houseton who lived in a small wooden "house" on the property. My mother recalled that she would visit Mrs Houseton often. Mrs Houseton would smoke her pipe and tell my little-girl mother stories from a rocking chair on her porch. "I don't remember Mrs Houseton ever doing work. I just remember her being kind to me. I assume her mother had been enslaved." What kind of trauma would it be (as a Black girl or woman in the Jim Crow era in rural Georgia) to have no other option but to remain on the property where one's mother had been called property, whether or not one was made to work there oneself?

Bill told us he'd drive us on the new road around to the other side of Drakies and we made a three-point turn near a huge mud puddle. "I've seen enough", my mother said when we passed a Target warehouse. We visited the family cemetery briefly, and then returned to Bill's so that I could get my car. I told them I'd meet them at the Quartermans' place.

A half hour before our meeting time with the Quartermans, I left Bill and my mother and drove to the Food Lion to buy some flowers, wondering what sort of arrangement was appropriate to offer the descendants of a man one's ancestor once enslaved.

Luckily there was only one choice. I propped the gallon-sized mason jar of wildflowers tied with a purple bow in the passenger seat next to me and drove slowly, past Bill's house, and then past the Quartermans' house as well, to make sure I had the address right. I drove a distance down the road until I could find a spot to turn back around. As I did, I questioned for the first time why I had set this meeting up. Was it more to help the Quarterman family, or to clear the Keller name? Or something else? How would this effort help me? Was "help" problematic here in every shape and way?

White saviorism refers to the acts of white people who help non-white people for self-serving reasons, the main reason being to absolve white people of guilt or shame or prove their own good-ness. I was sensitive to the lure of it, although I was not under the impression that I was saving anyone. Randy Quarterman could and did advocate for himself. I did not feel shame or guilt as I acted—shame is paralyzing, and unproductive—I felt hope. I hoped I was being respectful. *Am I overstepping?* I asked fre-quently as we worked together to email county officials and tried to get legal advice. *Do you want me to participate here, or should I hold back?* I felt vulnerable and open. But the questions of whom I was doing this work for and why unavoidably pro-duced multiple answers. I reassured myself that my intent was to bring truth to light about the racial wealth and opportunity gaps and the need for a conversation about reparations, and to help the Quartermans save and use the land they owned, not to prove my own worth or to prop up my latest writing project. I also heard a small voice beneath saying: "But maybe this does make you a better person" and "You know, you could write about this too."

#End#

Discussion questions and topics

- What powerful lessons did Randy learn from his family in Japan and in Korea that uniquely prepared him to be open to Sarah's inquiry when she reached out in 2019? What about the lessons Randy learned from his family in Savannah?

- What lessons did Sarah learn from her family that uniquely prepared her to want to engage with Randy in this work?

- Why do you think Sarah reached out to Randy / has involved herself in the work to uncover this story and act, where many other white people have not? Did she have a blueprint for what repair would look like?

- What connections, if any, do you see between Randy's teen years experiencing a loss of identity / identity crisis and anti-Black racism after his move to Savannah amid the crack epidemic, his struggle to reckon with his own Blackness and journey out of school and onto the streets, and Sarah's teen years experiencing depression and self-loathing as connected to family history and white supremacy and misogyny in America, her move to UCSB and discovery of a fertile and nourishing ground for finding her identity? Where does Sarah's white privilege show up? Or is there any situation in which it does *not* show up?

- Consider Sarah's belief that the legacy of slavery has contributed to mental illness or at least the epigenetics of shame, in her family and in other white families. Do you agree that this is possible? In what ways do you think white people in America need to heal from racism, if at all?

- Consider Randy's complicated path from Savannah to Atlanta and back, and into Job Corps, then the birth of his first son, and then joining the military. What was it like for Randy to go from one life to another? What were the personal and societal factors that contributed to each life change? Where do you think Randy's resiliency and ability to "pivot" and reshape his life repeatedly came from?

- Consider Sarah's Stanford engineering studies, connections made there, resulting work in a star tech company (Cisco Systems), being a part of a whole different world created as Silicon Valley took off. What did she experience as a white woman in that environment? What were her obvious privileges and were there any disadvantages for her? What did she understand at that point about her life trajectory and what were the factors that allowed her to "pivot" and interrogate her surroundings?

- Consider the very different ways in which Randy and Sarah experienced war, and the ways in which they reflect on the experiences today. What strikes you about the fact that they had very different options for participating in wars? Do you get the sense that they can talk openly about their perspectives on this? Why might that be possible for them when it isn't for so many Americans today?

- What role do the titles of the chapters in this book play? How might you read the book differently without them?

- Do you think white people who are descendants of enslavers owe personal reparations?

- Do you think the federal government owes some sort of national reparations to African Americans?

- What do reparations mean to you?

Additional resources and reading

You can read more about Randy and Sarah and their work to support Black education, Black land preservation, and Black art with The Reparations Project at reparationsproject.org.

Sarah and Randy are featured in a PBS documentary titled "The Cost of Inheritance" directed by Yoruba Richen. You can view the film and see a Study Guide associated with it here:

https://worldchannel.org/episode/america-reframed-the-cost-of-inheritance/

Reparations4slavery.com

Comingtothetable.org

Black Marxism: The Making of the Black Radical Tradition by Cedric Robinson

Administrations of Lunacy: Racism and the Haunting of American Psychiatry at the Milledgeville Asylum by Mab Segrest

The Willie Lynch Letter and the Making of a Slave by Willie Lynch

Learning from the Germans: Race and the Memory of Evil by Susan Neiman

Die Nigger Die by H. Rap Brown (Jamil Abdullah Al-Amin)

Transpacific Antiracism by Yuichiro Onishi

Stamped from the Beginning: The Definitive History of Racist Ideas in America by Ibram X. Kendi

Index

www.ingramcontent.com/pod-product-compliance
Lightning Source LLC
Chambersburg PA
CBHW070344270326
41926CB00017B/3972